LOVE SECRETS REVEALED

LOVE SECRETS

REVEALED

*What Happy Couples Know About
Having Great Sex, Deep Intimacy
and a Lasting Connection*

ALLEN BERGER, PH.D.
WITH MARY PALMER

Health Communications, Inc.
Deerfield Beach, Florida

www.hcibooks.com

The information in this book is not intended to replace counseling by a mental health professional. If the reader is experiencing troubling relationship issues, he or she should seek the advice of a mental health professional.

Cataloging-in-Publication information is available through the Library of Congress.

©2006 Allen Berger
ISBN 0-7573-0397-8

Publisher: Health Communications, Inc.
        3201 S.W. 15th Street
        Deerfield Beach, FL 33442–8190

Cover photo ©Joe Kingleigh/Getty Images
Cover and inside book design by Lawna Patterson Oldfield

CONTENTS

ACKNOWLEDGMENTS

*F*irst and foremost, I want to thank my immediate family and close friends who have stood by through thick and thin. Namely, Dymph, Danielle, Nicolas, Roger Andes, Russ Skoller and Damina Schiller. Your love and support are appreciated beyond words.

I also want to acknowledge how much I am indebted to my two mentors, Walter Kempler, M.D., and William C. Rader, M.D., for their personal and professional contributions to my career. You have taught me well and I love and respect you both.

Thanks to you, too, Jess. Your ongoing support is deeply appreciated.

Mary Palmer, your initial work helped this manuscript move beyond a dream to a reality.

To all my patients, I want to thank you for giving me the privilege of helping you in your troubled times.

And finally I want to thank Allison Janse and all of the staff at HCI. Your guidance, professionalism and support have been instrumental in creating a work that I am proud of: Thank you from the bottom of my heart.

FOREWORD

*F*or young people in the Western world, life as a couple has to be reinvented. Although you might have positive memories from the family you grew up in, there is little room for nostalgia. The basic values of a relationship between women and men have evolved in our society and will never be the same again. This doesn't mean that our parents and grandparents were "wrong"; merely that now is a different time.

As the author of this book points out, "Love is not enough!" The fact that I love my wife and at times experience this love in every fiber of my body and every aspect of my soul is wonderful for *me*—yet it does not give her anything per se. Our mutual love is certainly the basis of our relationship, but it does not create it. The creation takes place when we both succeed in transforming our loving emotions into loving behavior—behavior that the other person actually *experiences* as loving. How we do this without compromising our own integrity is the big question.

Dr. Berger's book clearly reveals that our work as family therapists has generated a body of important knowledge and

experience, which generally has proven helpful for people trying to make it work beyond the first few years when hormones
rule.

Love is the basis, but commitment the stone, from which the
foundation of a family is built. There are many people out there
who fall in love, but if they want to mature, they have to be willing to struggle in the context of a commitment. This personal
choice and desire forms the foundation of their commitment.

Since there are no such things as perfect societies or perfect
families, we all grow up tainted and twisted, and we all develop
behavioral patterns which do not serve our best interest as individuals or as partners. These self-destructive traits inevitably
become harmful to the people we love and who depend on us.
Because we love them, their pain will challenge our behavior and
force us to change or leave. Part of the commitment to another
person is the willingness to look inside and learn about the sometimes subtle difference between who we really are and the patterns that we so ingeniously created as we grew up in order to
cooperate with our parents. And this—precisely this—is only
possible within the emotional framework of a committed, love-
based relationship.

In this important book, Dr. Berger, drawing on his decades
of experience as a family therapist, demonstrates over and over
how conflicts and crises can lead to personal growth and
increased psychological health. Dr. Berger's book will be
equally valuable to new and experienced couples. I must warn
you that some of his information will make you uncomfortable, because it makes you question your own current behavior. While not easy to do, I encourage you to take this journey
with an open mind and heart. If you do, I am certain you will

find several important concepts that will help you in the challenging and rewarding journey of forging a loving and meaningful partnership.

Jesper Juul, acclaimed international family therapist and author of *Your Competent Child*

Human relationships always help us to carry on because they always presuppose further develop-ments, a future—and also because we live as if our only task was precisely to have relationships with other people.

—ALBERT CAMUS (1943)

Love is irrelevant in making a relationship work! It is not what keeps two people together. No amount of tender feelings or grand passion will guarantee a successful, long-term relationship.

We have glorified the role of love in relationships. We have been duped by song lyrics, happily-ever-after movies and greeting card verses that portray love as the essential ingredient for two people staying together. This idea has no basis in reality. In fact, most of the romantic notions of Western civilization destroy marriages and split couples.

We've all grown up with romantic ideals that are based on grossly misleading expectations and childlike myths. Yet we tenaciously hold on to these old ideas until it is too late. We often end up destroying what was once our most cherished possession. No one is immune. **We are cursed with unreasonable expectations and myths. Our ideas of love are based on romantic anachronisms: idealized and outdated ideas about love that poison chances for strong and successful relationships.**

Believe me, my clients do not like hearing that love is not the cure-all for ailing relationships. People argue with me when I tell them that love is not the answer to a couple's problems. Sometimes they yell. Other times they cry. I tell them they've built their lives on a falsehood. Such information is both powerful and upsetting. Most of us have lived our lives on the assumption that love brings success, harmony and understanding. Nothing could be further from the truth. The truth is that as a person becomes more important to you, it becomes more difficult to hold on to yourself in a relationship. Relationships are the sources of many kinds of trouble.

Before you hurl this book across the room and label me the Scrooge of the counseling profession, let me promise you that I do believe love is great. All human beings live to love and love to live. But it takes much more than love to build a good relationship.

When we first fall in love, we cherish the new relationship with our partner above everything else in our lives. Unfortunately, for most of us, this wonderful experience is short-lived. All too soon, we are faced with the practical challenges of making a relationship work.

Why can't we sustain this beautiful feeling throughout the entire life of the relationship? Is it nature's way of seducing us into reproducing? Is it really foolish to think that we can have a healthy, loving relationship, day in and day out?

If it is foolish, then I am proud to say that I am the greatest fool who ever lived. I believe that it is possible to create a healthy relationship that not only survives the daily drudgeries but thrives on the challenges that naturally flow from life in a long-term, committed relationship. I believe, with the proper skills and perspectives, couples can build relationships that sweeten their lives and enrich their souls.

Yet most of us have no idea of the skills and personal abilities necessary to form healthy relationships. We believe loving someone is enough, and the rest just happens naturally. This is an example of the ridiculous assumptions we've all been reared on.

How do we explain the thousands of failed relationships around us? Is it a lack of love? Is it the wrong kind of love? Falling out of love? These explanations are too simplistic. Love is great, but love is never enough to make a relationship work.

Healthy relationship skills are rarely modeled by parents and are not taught in high school or colleges. Television dramas create an unrealistic impression of how to struggle with conflict. We see problems resolved without much effort and little personal disclosure or vulnerability. In fact, any forms of healthy relationship skills are rarely modeled in our culture.

Who is to blame for a deficit that produces so much pain and suffering? Everyone and no one are to blame. Our parents communicated to us the best information available to them, and their parents did the same. But no one has all the answers, so the lesson is always incomplete. People can only pass on what they themselves have learned, and it's never enough.

This book is designed to supplement the information handed down to you. You will develop a basic understanding of how a healthy relationship functions, acquire new skills for interacting with your partner and, hopefully, gain a more mature and adult perspective on what it takes to make a relationship work.

Notice the emphasis is on skills and perspectives. No one can tell you what you need in a relationship. A good partnership is unique to each couple. A healthy relationship is never based on some ideal of what a relationship "should be like." A healthy relationship is created by how two people live together. It is the fruits of the labor of their love.

The purpose of this book is to empower you to become an expert in your particular relationship. In the chapters that follow, I will give you some basic information about the forces at work in every relationship. I will expose some major misconceptions of romantic love, challenge your expectations about relationships, and offer some guidelines to enhance your relationship and, if necessary, tell you how to encourage a reluctant spouse to join you in therapy. But no one can tell you what you need in a relationship. That is up to you.

In order to provide you with some idea of my qualifications I offer you the following. First, I am writing as a man who has been married twice. The concepts and suggestions in this book are ones that I myself have experimented with and found valuable. I am a true believer in sharing what I learned through the pain and personal struggles I have experienced in my relationships.

Second, I am writing to you as a psychologist. I have synthesized in this book the information I have gained during my education and training. I was fortunate enough to work with Walter Kempler, M.D., a pioneer in the field of family therapy, and I will share many of the insights gained from my training.

And last, but just as important, I will pass on the understanding I have gleaned from over thirty years of clinical experience with thousands of men and women who were struggling to create more mutually satisfying relationships.

Let me add one caveat before we begin. Don't swallow whole the information in this or any other book simply because it is written by a "professional." I'd much rather see you taste it and chew it up well before swallowing. If you're still not sure it's for you, experiment with the concepts. Your own experiences will tell you whether or not these suggestions may be useful tools in your life. Remember, there is no such thing as a failed experiment. All experiences, regardless of their outcomes, provide important information.

CHAPTER 1

The Stuff You Have to Understand for the Rest of This Book to Make Sense

ong-term commitment to an intimate relationship with one person of whatever sex is an essential need that people have in order to breed the qualities out of which nurturant thought can rise.

—GERDA LERNER (1981)

Love in Today's Social Context

Pat and Jane are in their mid-thirties. Jane worked during the first part of their relationship and supported the family while Pat attended law school. After Pat graduated and passed the bar exam, they started expanding their family and today enjoy two beautiful children. For the past

1

several years, Pat has been focusing on building his career, spending long hours at the office, going above and beyond the call of duty, to impress the partners of the firm. Jane's new job is raising her two children and managing their recently purchased home. This shift in their individual roles was not easy. Pat has been having trouble connecting to his wife after a full day's work; he's often exhausted and doesn't know how to get close to her. He helps her out because she seems so tired and drained by caring for their two young children throughout the day. But something is missing; he is helpful, but disconnected from the woman he loves. He suffers in silence, as do most men. He never developed the ability to tell his wife what he wants; his personal language is poorly developed because in his family of origin his father focused on being a provider rather than a participant.

Jane also contributes to their problems. She is unhappy with their connection, but because Pat works so hard she swallows her unfulfilled desires in order to not burden Pat. She tries to remain loyal to her love for Pat, but she never learned that mature love means to having loyalty to herself too. So she remains silent. They are both suffering from a lack of intimacy. In Jane's family of origin, she learned to please others at her own expense as a way of expressing love. A deadly combination for this young couple, wouldn't you agree? The good news is that they have reached out for help. They want more than just a marriage in name only; they want a passionate, loving connection. They are not alone.

Today the forces that join two people are extremely complex, but love has emerged as the central concern for the first time in the history of Western civilization. What does this mean to you and me in the twenty-first century?

I believe we are in the midst of a dramatic social change. We are moving toward a more personal and authentic consciousness. Self-help books now fill a whole section at the bookstore. Reality TV dominates much of the programming on television as we watch people from all walks from life struggle with their personal lives. We watch to see how they get along with friends, lovers, husbands and wives and to witness how they face real, practical issues and difficulties. Our willingness to study human interactions resulted in the Civil Rights movement, the women's movement and the men's movement—and it continues today.

Our increased life spans present special stresses to our relationships. Because of advances in medical science, we are faced with learning how to love a person for a longer period of time. Today a couple's marriage may last two decades more than their parents'. The challenge becomes how to stay connected and passionate for the entire course of the marriage.

What all this means is that love no longer exists merely as a courtship ritual that withers after the first year of marriage. An altogether different sort of love is emerging: a love that is based on individuality and integrity, rather than on social dictates or emotional dependency. Erich Fromm anticipated the character of this type of love when he stated that, **"Mature love is union with the preservation of integrity."** This is the type of love we need to embrace in the twenty-first century.

I'm certain that the romantics reading this book are jumping for joy. However, this notion of love is not an idealized love. It is a love that springs from striving to create a mutually satisfying relationship. It is not solely created by chemistry. It is created by learning how to hold on to yourself and stay connected to your partner. It is a love grounded in developing an understanding forged from the conflict that eventually reveals the higher purpose that brought you and your partner together. It is a love created by learning how to live together with integrity and respect. It is a love that is strengthened by struggling with your partner in a way that requires authenticity.

The Natural Therapeutic Value of Relationships

Sigmund Freud's seminal work in psychology has had a tremendous impact on how we understand ourselves and our behavior. I don't want to burden you with textbook details, but there are a couple of important insights that directly affect our understanding of what happens in relationships. Let me give you an example.

Imagine a little girl abandoned by her alcoholic father, not because he wasn't physically present, but because he was often too drunk to interact in a meaningful way with any members of the family. At sixteen she runs away and marries her boyfriend. In the course of their marriage, he begins drinking. She can't believe the love of her life is doing the same thing to her that her father did. She gets angry and attacks him about his drinking, which further drives him away.

Why does a woman who was abandoned by her father as a child grow up and marry a man who abandons her? Why does a man divorce a cold, critical woman only to marry someone who is her psychological twin? According to Freud, all of our behavior has a psychological cause, but often the cause is hidden within our unconscious.

Freud believed that the psyche develops out of the resolution of conflict. If conflict resolution is successful, at whatever particular stage of psychological development, then we move on to the next stage with few or no residual problems. However, sometimes we get stuck at a particular stage of development that destines us to apply the same solution over and over again, whether it works or not. It's like the needle of a phonograph stuck in the groove of a record.

Go back to the example of the abandoned woman. Let's imagine her husband dies in an industrial accident. She is free! There is a second courtship and the woman remarries. Six months later her new husband begins acting very similarly to her first husband. According to Freud, this woman will be stuck in this painful cycle of emotional neglect all her life.

I am much more optimistic than Freud! I believe, as do many humanistic and existential psychologists, that our mate selection has an underlying positive intention. *I see an inherent wisdom to our behavior that we often overlook or discount.* I am convinced all our behavior is a natural extension of an inner urge to grow up and move toward greater emotional and spiritual maturity.

Therefore, we choose a partner who will stir us to change in necessary ways. Carl Whitaker, M.D., and Augustus Napier, Ph.D., call this the "wisdom of the unconscious." Here's what this means. We select a partner who is going to cause us the "right kind of trouble." *We pick someone who, by his or her very nature, will furnish us with an opportunity to master the as-yet unaltered, to encourage us to give a voice to the as-yet unspeakable, to insist that we take another step forward in the endless pursuit of personal development and personal integrity.*

This is the natural therapeutic value of a relationship. It is as if our partners are angels, heaven-sent, to inspire us toward maturity and integrity (wholeness). Their help usually comes from the most unexpected directions and in the most unexpected ways. Typically, growth comes from the pain and frustration they help create in the relationship.

In the example of the woman who feels abandoned, her husband's behavior is bringing her emotional and spiritual wound to the foreground of her life. She now has the opportunity to face her pain and begin what will be a lifetime endeavor of healing this pain and learning to hold on to her self regardless of her husband's behavior. She will eventually realize that she learned how to abandon herself a long time ago. And eventually she will learn how to take care of herself—the next step in her personal development.

Sadly, for most couples, the therapeutic value of a relationship is more of an idea in a psychologist's book than a reality. Why does this happen? There are two reasons: Either we do not respect and acknowledge the depth of wisdom that operates within us, and/or we lack the skills that would help us realize the inherent worth of our relationships. Thus, the original good judgment and potential that joined us with our partner are rarely realized. We lose sight of the bigger picture and become confused, frustrated, disheartened, angry, sad or hopeless. The relationship deteriorates; we distance ourselves from our partners; and we sometimes divorce or just give up and remain in an unfulfilling relationship.

Losing sight of the relationship's purpose is one of the most common causes of divorce. Many people get divorced because they no longer see the value of their relationship and their love dies.

Recognizing that there is unrealized value in your relationship may provide you a vision worthy of facing and struggling with your circumstances. When you integrate this broader horizon into your understanding, suffering becomes more tolerable because it is seen as necessary to help you take the next step on your personal journey. Emotional pain does not have to be a permanent condition.

Understanding the personal significance of your pain can enable you to face hardships and discover important and critical information from your experience. I hope you can keep this in mind whenever you are struggling with difficulties in your relationship.

When we accept and digest the challenges we have created in our lives and relationships, we become more complete and move closer to becoming whole, becoming the best we can be.

When we are on the "right path," we will thrive and our relationships will flourish. A healthy relationship is like a timely serving of soul food. It feeds our spiritual hunger. Eaten and digested properly, our souls will sing with ecstasy and inspiration. Sex becomes electric, encounters enriching, dialogue meaningful. When we approach our relationships from this perspective, negative emotions offer opportunities for intimacy.

The Cruel Legacy of Unconditional Love

When I speak of the therapeutic value of relationships, I am not describing a process in which partners gradually shed their humanness to become haloed saints fit only to hobnob with seraphim and cherubim among clouds of unconditional love. In fact, I believe that the term "unconditional love" has further complicated the issues involved in establishing and maintaining a mature and healthy relationship.

The notion that we can love a partner unconditionally, without regard to anything our partner says or does, would require us to completely deny our humanity. Because the "unconditional love" movement has taught us we are "selfish" unless we suppress our needs and expectations in order to perfectly love our partner, many of us go through life feeling stuck between a rock and a hard place. We continue to have expectations of our partners even though we've been taught expectations are wrong. We keep on getting angry and disappointed although we're told anger is "negative." We struggle with the "I" that keeps popping up in our relationships.

I do not believe any relationship is healthy in which self-sacrifice is a major requirement, and self-sacrifice is a requirement for unconditional love. I will be discussing this further in Chapter Two. The important thing to remember right now is that **there must be room for both partners in a mutually satisfying relationship**.

The vision I have for a healthy relationship is similar to that expressed by the British psychiatrist Anthony Storr when he described the ideal marriage. He stated, "A happy marriage perhaps represents the ideal of human relationship—a setting in which each partner, while acknowledging the need of the other, feels free to be what he or she by nature is: a relationship in which instinct as well as intellect can find expression; in which giving and taking are equal; in which each accepts the other, and I confronts Thou." This ideal is a great goal to strive for, but I don't want you to be fooled into thinking that this kind of emotional climate is easy to create. It's not. But there is great value in striving for such a wonderful and authentic union.

The Balancing Act in All Relationships

The confrontation of "I and Thou" (me and you) in a relationship requires the ability to balance two issues that naturally arise in the course of life: (1) the desire to join, cooperate with and please your partner, and (2) the pursuit of your own individuality. Both of these forces are deeply rooted in our lives. Let's take a look at these in more detail.

Cooperation and the desire to please are essential to survival. Our desire to cooperate and please is first manifested in an infant's relationship with its mother. The mother's breasts fill with milk for the baby, and the infant's feeding relieves the pressure in the mother's chest. Mother and child are cooperating and ensuring the immediate survival of the child, as well as creating the deep attachment necessary for parents to withstand all of the frustrations that inevitably occur over eighteen to twenty-one years. Who hasn't fallen in love with a newborn's innocent smile?

Cooperation is a prerequisite for successful social adaptation as an adult. We are social animals. The individual who is unable to cooperate is typically considered an outcast and often lives on the fringes of society. Some anthropologists have argued that the complex social interactions between human beings fueled the evolutionary engine that eventually created language and the human brain, making cooperation possible.

However, cooperation alone does not assure personal success. The second major force in our lives is the pursuit of our individuality. There is an intrinsic motivation to become all you can be. We desire to follow our own paths, assert our needs and wants, master problems, find solutions, and discover our purpose in life.

When we balance these two forces, we are functioning with integrity. Integrity, as it is used throughout this book, is concerned with wholeness and maturity. People who function with integrity honor what is important to them at any particular moment. They do not lose themselves to social customs or peer pressure, nor do they dismiss the social demands or rules of a situation. People with integrity consider all of this information and integrate these considerations into their responses.

This awareness facilitates the integration of our individuality and our desire to please. As you can see, integrity involves self-concern, but don't mistake self-concern with selfishness. Selfishness has nothing to do with the self-concern that is necessary to balance these two forces.

The pursuit of integrity is always at work in our lives. We seek information. We desire to learn. In fact, we create situations in our lives that provide us with opportunities to learn. We are constantly struggling with our desire to please and our desire to follow our own directives, and this struggle will always be most evident in important relationships.

While our desire to maintain our integrity is always present, unfortunately it is not always honored. Either we honor our desire to please at the expense of our individuality or we honor our self at the expense of our desire to cooperate. In either case, we lose our integrity and therefore limit our relationships and fail to realize our potential as people.

Integrity also has a quality to it that moves us toward closure or resolution. If something is incomplete, we want to bring it to closure. The nature of integrity spurs us toward wholeness. Let's see how these forces manifest themselves in our primary relationships.

In a primary relationship, you cocreate an atmosphere that determines how you, as a couple, balance your competing needs for cooperation and individuality. What is said between you and your partner, and what is not said, creates invisible rules that govern the interactions, the level of intimacy and the dynamics of your relationship. These rules create a social structure for your relationship that encourages or discourages integrity. How you respond to your partner's desire to please, how you respond to your partner's individuality, how you encourage your partner to have his or her voice and how you balance these two forces in your life are some of the ways you create the social structure that governs your relationship.

Unfortunately, couples often create an atmosphere that undermines the healthy management of the drive for cooperation and the drive for individuality. When a relationship is imbalanced or skewed, it seems that one party in the relationship falls out of bed on one side, while the other partner falls out on the other.

For example, Russ and Cathy came into their first counseling session with me with a common complaint. Cathy said up front, "I am the giver and my partner is the taker." Russ countered, "I don't ask you to fuss over me. Sometimes I feel like I'm married to my mother." Clearly, Cathy was trying to please and cooperate to the point of losing sight of her self in the marriage and she was quite resentful. On the other hand, Russ was quite willing to accept her sacrifice.

Typically a person adopts one side of these two forces as a

basic solution to life. You either become a people-pleaser or self-centered. If you are a people-pleaser, you move toward your partner and try to become whatever you think he or she wants you to be. You determine how you are going to behave based on your perception of what your partner wants. You lack an inner compass that points the way; your direction is determined by your partner's needs.

Conversely, if you are self-centered, you fear losing yourself and so avoid or minimize intimacy. Your self-centeredness obstructs your capacity to have empathy and therefore you are out of touch with your partner's needs or desires. The truth is that you are as emotionally dependent as the people-pleaser. Your partner is too important because you do not know how to hold on to yourself and stay connected.

In a successful relationship, we please our mate without compromising our own individuality; we strive to maintain our integrity. We learn to honor our desires and yet respond to our partner's needs and desires. We respond as allies to our partners, without losing sight of what is important to us, and then we work together to discover a solution to our unique problems while also guarding against our partner's submission or false compliance.

In order for a relationship to be based on who each person is, rather than on an ideal of what a relationship should be like, we need to hold on to ourselves and inform our mates how to be our partners, to let them know what we need. And at the same time we must encourage our partner to reveal his or her needs to us, too.

As the saying goes, "You can't always get what you want, but if you try sometimes, you just might find you get what you need." It is impossible to tell your partner what is important to you if you don't understand what is important to yourself. **The more self-knowledge you have, the better partner you can be.** Therefore, an important aspect of becoming a good partner is confronting yourself and understanding what you want, and then being able to communicate your desires to your partner. I'll discuss this more later.

Let's now turn our attention to disappointment and failure and how they are addressed in your relationship.

Whose Fault Is It Anyway?

Blame is rampant in relationships today as couples search for explanations of their ongoing failures to make their relationship or marriage work. Blaming each other, our parents or their parents is futile. Rarely will it lead you to a place where you can heal a wound or truly learn how to be a better partner. Here is why.

Blame is based on linear thinking. The logic goes something like this: A causes B, so therefore we must do something about A if we want to change the outcome. This way of thinking permeates our lives. Our society and culture are based on this type of an approach to life. Family therapists have challenged this assumption over the past fifty years, and the results have revolutionized psychotherapy.

There has been a shift in our thinking that is extremely helpful in relationships. I will refer to this as "systems thinking." It is based on the idea that you are jointly creating the social reality of your relationship. Neither of you is to blame, and yet both of you are at fault. **There are no victims, only volunteers.**

As you will see throughout this book, I am strongly committed to this idea. I believe it is an incredibly powerful idea because it frees you from being a victim. It empowers you. You influence your situation whether or not you realize it. If I am right about this, it means you can have a greater impact on a situation than you may have ever believed. It also means that your partner doesn't have to change for you to change your relationship; once you begin to change, the relationship will change. It has to. Once you change what you are doing in your relationship, the pattern of interaction between you and your partner will be different.

Confronting Yourself

We live in a painphobic culture. We hate pain, especially psychological pain. We avoid facing our anxieties, shortcomings and limitations. We have difficulty being rigorously honest with ourselves and therefore turn away from important personal realities. We have selective inattention and try to avoid seeing things about ourselves, our families of origin or our current relationships that need serious attention. I have said to many of my patients, "You can pay me now or pay me later!" It is a basic principle of our human makeup that brings unresolved issues back into the foreground of our consciousness time and time again until they are addressed and resolved. Essentially, you can run, but you can never hide.

Finding the courage to face yourself is the most important thing you can do for your relationship. The more you understand yourself and where you have difficulty holding on to yourself, the better you will be able to:

➠ identify where you are not functioning with integrity;

➠ become aware of how you are letting your anxieties and shortcomings drive or immobilize you;

➠ see how you fail to soothe yourself when you are upset or anxious;

➠ address your emotional dependency and how it impacts your relationship;

➠ face personal issues that interfere with your becoming the kind of partner and person you want to be; and finally,

➠ focus your time and energy on becoming a better partner.

Putting the Information to Work

Truly knowing yourself and confronting your personal issues is an important step in improving your relationship. But insight without action is merely an intellectual exercise and not the beginning of a real, deep, personal transformation. The key word to remember is "integration." What you learn needs to become integrated into your life. It needs to be applied to how you treat and interact with yourself and your partner.

Learning about yourself and understanding your personal issues will allow you to identify the personal baggage you have dragged into your relationship. It will help you identify what you need to change to become the partner you want to be.

To help you confront yourself, in the next three chapters I have identified some of the romantic myths, unreasonable expectations and destructive communication patterns prevalent in our lives today. Be honest with yourself and stop running away from your issues. It's your only chance to turn things around in your life.

Now let's jump into the water and have some fun. Grab a brand new highlighter and a pen (in case you want to mark up a section that is particularly relevant to your life or make some notes), and prepare to be as honest with yourself as possible. In the next chapter we begin exposing common myths about relationships.

CHAPTER 2

Shattering Romantic Myths

M yths which are believed in tend to become true.

—George Orwell

Myths are beliefs whose truth we accept uncritically. By the time we become adults, we've absorbed many beliefs about romantic relationships both from our culture and our personal experiences. However, we do not identify these teachings as myths. For us, they're the truth with a capital **"T."** They've become a portable reality we carry into every situation we encounter in our life journey.

We're like exhausted travelers dragging a huge suitcase with no rollers through an endless airport as we struggle with these myths. Tired as we are, we never think to stop and check the contents. We've picked up myths all along the way—some family hand-me-downs, others that we've stuffed inside the suitcase ourselves. Whatever the source, once we've crammed them into our bag, we don't examine them critically.

Before exploring new information about the nature of romantic relationships, we must evaluate those myths to determine whether they are true for our lives today. When we discard myths, we are eliminating dangerous ideas that can destroy even very good relationships.

In this chapter, I will discuss ten harmful myths that are common in our society.

1. Love is the solution.
2. If you really loved me, you'd _____
   _____ (fill in the blank).
3. When you're in a healthy relationship, you do not argue or fight.
4. If I am in a good relationship, I won't feel lonely.
5. You must think alike to have a good relationship.
6. There is such a thing as a perfect relationship.
7. A good relationship is based on compromise.
8. We need to work harder at our relationship.
9. Desire equals ability.
10. Till death do us part!

You may find that some of these myths express beliefs you have held. Others may not apply to you. The important task is to look and question. The better you understand yourself and the body of convictions you hold, the better the relationship you can shape with someone else.

LOVE IS THE SOLUTION.

THE REALITY: Contrary to all our cultural conditioning and expectations, love is *irrelevant* in solving relationship problems.

There is no question that being in love is a powerful and beautiful human experience. It is also true that love is an essential component of a successful romantic relationship. But love alone can't fix a couple's problems any more than love can enable a person to develop the musculature and lung capacity to scale Mount Everest.

In fact, the idea that problems are caused by lack of love is often the *source* of a couple's difficulties. Here is a situation that developed when Rick and Shirley came to me to save their nine-year marriage. Rick, a thirty-four-year-old building contractor, was convinced that lack of love was the problem in his marriage with Shirley. In fact, Shirley had told him so one Sunday after he'd come home from sailing with his two boat partners.

Rick told me, "I went all-out on a 'love' campaign. I brought her a bunch of lilacs. I took her to the new Greek restaurant she'd wanted to go to. I made her coffee in the morning. And for a while things seemed to be better, but then in a few weeks she was saying again that I just didn't love her enough."

I've met many clients who have been frustrated in this way. They attempt to solve problems in the relationship by embarking on an intense crusade of unremitting kindness and consideration—but I've never seen this strategy help in the long run.

It's like taking aspirin for a broken bone. It eases the pain, but the bone still needs to be set. Lack of love usually has nothing to do with difficulty in a relationship. In therapy Rick realized that Shirley wasn't talking about love, she was talking about respect. Shirley experienced Rick as disrespectful, and she didn't know how to take care of herself when he treated her this way.

She had an idea that crippled her ability to take care of herself in a relationship. She believed Rick should take care of her *because* he loved her. This is one of the greatest myths prevalent in our society today when it comes to intimacy. We have confused emotional dependency with love. In my opinion, Rick was too important to Shirley. She gave him too much authority in her life; he had the power to make her feel good or bad. This emotional dependency leads to an expectation that intimacy and love should be based on reciprocal behavior: "You should treat me the way I want you to in order for me to feel close to you." Dr. David Schnarch referred to this as "other based intimacy." This type of intimacy is based on emotional dependency, not love.

Let's look at how this idea was applied to treating Rick and Shirley. Rick needed to be confronted about his behavior. He was disrespectful, and I didn't hesitate to discuss my impression with him. Respect is the minimum requirement of love. But Rick's being disrespectful was compounded by the fact that Shirley didn't know how to hold on to herself when interacting with Rick.

She didn't speak up for herself because she believed that Rick shouldn't act this way if he truly loved her. Her myth about love made her impotent. She lost her voice in the relationship because she was dependent on Rick to take care of her.

Rick seemed to be genuinely unaware that he was cutting Shirley off when she would try to talk with him or, worse yet, tell her there really wasn't anything to be concerned about when she expressed a particular concern. He was dismissing Shirley's feelings.

Once Shirley started to hold on to herself and better assert herself, she quit taking his behavior personally and they started to improve their communication. She would challenge Rick whenever she felt disrespected by saying something like, "When you talk to me like that I feel disrespected. I want you to consider my point before you just dismiss my idea."

A lack of love was no longer the issue for Shirley. Now the issue was keeping her integrity, which she rightly viewed as her responsibility and not Rick's. Shirley kept her integrity by setting appropriate boundaries with Rick and not tolerating disrespectful behavior.

Solving a problem in a relationship usually involves addressing emotional dependency and how it is affecting solid communication skills, respect, empathy, win/win negotiations, humility and the ability to treat your partner as an ally. **Love makes a struggle worthwhile, but it cannot give us the ability to successfully struggle with these issues; learning how to hold on to yourself takes practice.**

MYTH 2:

IF YOU REALLY LOVED ME, YOU'D
_____ (FILL IN THE BLANK).

THE REALITY: Love does not govern the behavior of people. In fact, we often save our worst behavior for those we love.

There are two problems with this myth. The first occurs because we are interpreting our partner's behavior personally, as if the behavior reflects the level of his or her feelings toward us. Do any of the following phrases sound familiar?

"If you really loved me, you'd _____

➠ stop being stingy with money."

➠ be nice to my mother."

➠ never raise your voice to me."

➠ get a job."

➠ clean the hair out of the drain after you shower."

➠ quit gambling or drinking."

➠ not have an affair."

The assumption underlying this myth is that love will make a person behave in a desired manner. This is absolute nonsense.

Over the years I have treated many couples in which one spouse suffered from chemical dependency. Frances was thirty-two years old when she came in for what she bitterly described as "solo marriage counseling." She told me her husband, Stan, had a drinking problem and had just been fired for the second time. "He swears he loves me, but he won't even come for counseling," Frances said in despair. As far as Frances was concerned, Stan's failure to deal with his drinking problem was proof that he did not love her.

I told her that Stan's behavior was entirely normal—for an alcoholic! And that he was right—his drinking truly had nothing to do with whether he loved her. Eventually, Frances did an intervention that involved herself, Stan's parents and his sister. They shared with Stan their concern about his well-being. They shared with him how much they loved him and how they saw his drinking ruining his life.

Stan responded positively to the intervention, as most alcoholics do, and went to Cumberland Heights, an outstanding treatment center for alcoholism and other drug addictions in Nashville, Tennessee. He has achieved over a year of sobriety.

Today Frances has come to realize that both Stan's drinking and his recovery are completely separate from his love for her. Her love was an inspiration for Stan to begin recovery, but it had nothing to do with his drinking. He drank because he had a medical disease: he was an alcoholic.

In order to have a healthy relationship, we must stop taking personally everything our partner does. Only then can we truly see our lover as the person he or she is.

The paradox at work here is that once we stop taking things personally, we can get more personal. We will be able to recognize our partners' struggles with life and the difficulty they are having being a good partner, rather than seeing their behavior as a reflection of how they feel about us.

The second concern here is that love does not destine a person to act in a desirable manner. Why can such a beautiful feeling be the harbinger of a nightmare? Because our ideas about love are **often contaminated by emotional dependency that often started with the lessons we learned about love while we were growing up**. These confusions are always lurking below the surface of a romantic relationship. And once the relationship moves past the honeymoon stage, the painful and poignant issues associated with love surface. So instead of love naturally deepening our intimacy, you can, in fact, expect the opposite to happen. As a person becomes more important to you, your ability to hold on to yourself will undergo a greater challenge, a challenge that most of us have difficulty meeting. The more trouble you have holding on to yourself, the more problems you will experience. Because of this dynamic, love can bring out our worst demons. This is why we often treat those we love worse than we do strangers.

Take John, for instance. He was physically and verbally abused as a child. For John, love was confused with abuse. In fact, at some level John didn't believe someone cared for him unless the person was abusive.

When Suzy married John, she felt that she was the luckiest woman in the world. John was the sweetest man she had ever met. He charmed Suzy with a whirlwind courtship, and six months later they married. It was then the relationship began to deteriorate. John seemed to change. He began acting in a way that provoked very strong feelings of rage in Suzy. He became very passive. He would not communicate with Suzy, and he would frustrate her by forgetting to follow through on his promises. She had never hit a man before, but she was beginning to fantasize about physically pounding John into the ground.

When they finally showed up in my office, Suzy was furious and almost shaking with rage as she described the decline of their marriage. She felt duped. John was not the man he presented himself to be.

John was also very confused. He was aware of how he had changed, but he had no insight into what caused this sudden change of behavior.

During the course of therapy, John started to explore his emotional dependency and how it made it difficult for him to be the person he wanted to be. The exploration of John's emotional dependency and the emotional wounds he suffered in his childhood began to shed some light on the difficulty he was having in holding on to himself in this marriage. In the sessions that occurred over the next year, he discussed several episodes he suffered as a child that illustrated the terrible confusion about love. For instance, he recalled one afternoon when, upon coming home from school, his mother was terribly abusive. Earlier that day, his mother had started drinking after a vicious argument with her husband. She must have been fuming all day long. When she entered John's room, she noticed that John left out some items of clothing on his bed. This usually wasn't a big deal, but on this day it gave her an excuse to release her frustration on her son. As she whipped him with a thin leather belt, she declared her love for him. She reasoned that he needed to be taught a lesson about being neat and clean because she loved him. His father also criticized him relentlessly under the guise of love. It is no wonder that John never learned to hold on to himself. His desire to please and cooperate with his parents was constantly frustrated. He survived and cooperated with their expectations by becoming passive. He learned to disappear. This is how he cooperated with his parents—and it also lessened his chance of being beaten or criticized. Whenever he did express his discontent, he was sure to camouflage it.

John frustrated Suzy because as she became more important to him, he had trouble holding on to himself. Instead of discussing his fears and reactions, he disappeared, just as he did as a child.

We do not alter deeply ingrained behaviors because we love or don't love a person. All of us come to relationships with behaviors that were established before we met our mate. So what can you expect from love in a relationship? **Love can create a backdrop that makes change desirable, but love alone is not enough to generate a personal transformation.** Change takes a commitment to one's personal development, something that is all too often ignored in our modern society. Unfortunately, we are not living in a culture that promotes wisdom or encourages us to take a personal journey of self-discovery. It's your job to instill a personal commitment to growth and development into your life, whether or not your partner does likewise.

John and Suzy struggled through several years to find a better way to be with each other and to treat themselves better. Their efforts paid off and helped them learn how to stay connected and keep sight of their individuality. Suzy no longer wants to pound her husband into the ground.

MYTH 3:

WHEN YOU'RE IN A HEALTHY RELATIONSHIP, YOU DO NOT ARGUE OR FIGHT.

THE REALITY: Loving hurts, and good loving hurts a lot!

Serenity is only one aspect of a vital relationship. If you want permanent peace and quiet, take up residence in a cemetery. You won't find it in a healthy relationship. A healthy relationship is forged from the fires of marital conflict and discord.

The problem is that some people view any form of conflict as negative. Gwen and Gil came to me after four years of marriage. Gwen described the problem as one of communication. "Gil never wants to hear anything bad. As soon as I bring up a problem, he's like Mount Rushmore. His face turns to granite. He says I'm attacking him."

Gil countered, "I work hard all day. I want to relax when I get home. That's not asking too much."

Gil had come to view any conflict as negative. As a child he heard constant bickering between his parents that resulted in casualties, not resolutions. As a result he developed black-and-white or absolute thinking: arguing is bad; peace is good. Therefore, he reasoned, if he and Gwen avoided fighting, they would have a perfect marriage.

Actually his demands for peace were destroying their marriage. Gwen thought Gil didn't care what was happening in their lives, and it's easy to see how she came to misinterpret his behavior. This idea is often expressed to explain what is wrong with a relationship—when the opposite is true. The most trouble shows up in a relationship when a person is too important to another person.

After several sessions, both Gwen and Gil recognized that the message behind his avoidance was really, "I'm afraid. I don't know how to deal with what you're telling me. I want to please you, and I can't bear the thought that I'm not."

As Gil learned to say these words to Gwen out loud, their relationship improved enormously. Gwen also looked at how critical she became toward Gil. Needless to say, her criticism was also a part of their problem. Eventually Gil learned to stop defending himself against inaccurate criticisms from Gwen.

As they were able to face each other with these issues, their relationship improved. This type of healthy interaction between partners is what I refer to as "grinding." The process is tough, **but grinding is naturally therapeutic and will polish the bond between two people to great brilliance**.

Through this type of grinding, Gil and Gwen learned much about each other: how to hold on to themselves, and how to meet each other in a better way—a way that would create a mutually satisfying relationship. They also came to view their differences as beneficial, which helped them struggle in a win/win spirit. You'll read about how to create a win/win relationship later, in chapter 5.

IF I AM IN A GOOD RELATIONSHIP, I WON'T FEEL LONELY.

THE REALITY: A relationship can only distract you from a sense of loneliness. It does not cure it. The cure for your loneliness will come from developing a better relationship with yourself.

"Lone" means "single or unaccompanied," but the condition of lone-li-ness does not stem from lack of company. Loneliness springs from the failure of a person's relationship with him- or herself, and this aching emptiness is one of the most painful emotions we humans experience. Relationships may distract from a sense of loneliness for a time, but they will not cure it.

I met Marilyn and Lyle three and a half years into their relationship. Lyle was on the verge of leaving and had only agreed to come for counseling after Marilyn threatened to cut her wrists. Lyle's anger at being manipulated glinted throughout his account.

"At first I was flattered that she was so much in love with me," he said. "She'd call me several times a day, come by my apartment all the time. I knew she was a little insecure, but I loved her and I figured that once we moved in together, she'd recognize that I really did love her. Instead, she got more and more demanding, and now I feel like I'm her prisoner."

Individuals who believe in the myth that another person can cure their loneliness cannot form successful relationships. At first, their desire to be with their partner all the time is endearing. The partner feels special and important. As time passes, however, this special feeling turns into resentment and dislike. When the lover senses the beloved pulling away, he becomes fearful and even more demanding, which in turn provokes further withdrawal. Here again, we see the harmful effects of emotional dependence.

Marilyn's loneliness spawned a dependency on her relationship with Lyle as intense as an addiction to heroin. Because Marilyn had not achieved a healthy relationship with herself, she looked to Lyle to "fix" her, something neither he nor any other lover could do, and when he told her he planned to leave, she became frantic. A dependent partner truly believes he or she cannot live without the other person and clings to the relationship with the desperation of an exhausted swimmer caught in a riptide.

Today Marilyn continues to come for individual therapy to learn how to be "self-supportive." Lyle has ended their relationship, but it is Marilyn's hope that one day, when she has a surer sense of self, she will be able to form a successful romantic relationship. But the reality is that there is nothing like being in a relationship to prepare you for that relationship. A relationship prepares you for a relationship like nothing else can.

MYTH 5:

YOU MUST THINK ALIKE
TO HAVE A GOOD RELATIONSHIP.

THE REALITY: A good relationship is based on accepting differences and finding a value in these differences.

A young newlywed once told me in despair, "We just don't see eye to eye on anything."

"What do you disagree about?" I asked.

"Everything," she cried. "He brushes his teeth with hot water!"

Upheaval over dental hygiene makes us laugh, but in truth most of us believe our loved ones should think and act just like we do in everything—from how we brush our teeth to what we theorize about afterlife. We exert pressure, sometimes subtly, sometimes overtly, on our mates to mirror our own thoughts and feelings.

Incredibly painful conflicts can erupt when partners with different personality styles come together. Melissa and Jerry provide a classic example of marriage between a "feeling'" woman and a "thinking" man.

During counseling sessions Melissa often accused Jerry of being a coldhearted scientist (he was a computer programmer). In retaliation, Jerry repeatedly referred to Melissa as an "airhead" who refused to base important decisions on facts. In working with Jerry and Melissa, I focused on helping them understand their different personality styles and that neither way of perceiving the world is "right." Both orientations, thinking and feeling, have strengths and weaknesses. The important task for them was to accept and value each other's different approaches.

All too often we perceive the differences between us as threats to our couplehood. If we belittle or condemn our partner's individual style and attribute bad motives to them, we make matters worse.

No relationship can flourish if there is not enough room for both parties. This means that we must learn to respect differences so each person feels welcome, desirable and valuable.

The dynamic behind this pressure for conformity is once again emotional dependency. Differences between emotionally immature couples are experienced as threats because they illustrate that they are separate from each other. Their belief is that, "If we don't feel the same way, we can't be intimate." The opposite is really true. You cannot experience a deep and profound sense of intimacy unless you are able to hold on to yourself while staying connected to your partner.

Eventually Jerry learned how to value his wife's concern for how people are feeling. She, on the other hand, learned to accept Jerry's focus on analyzing data systematically as his personality style, and she stopped taking his behavior personally. This shift in her perception allowed her to hear what Jerry was really saying rather than filtering it through her pain. Their differences became assets rather than liabilities.

THERE IS SUCH A THING AS A
PERFECT RELATIONSHIP.

THE REALITY: We are a nation obsessed with being perfect. There are no perfect relationships. Instead of striving for perfection, we should be striving to have a healthy and genuine relationship.

Recently I attended a party for a couple celebrating their golden wedding anniversary. As I neared the husband and wife in the receiving line, I heard a guest gush, "You're the perfect couple," and both the man and woman turned to wink at me. I had treated them in therapy two years previously when they came close to breaking up. Even surrounded by gold and white streamers and plenty of hearts and flowers, they would not pretend their marriage was perfect.

There are no perfect relationships. You are setting yourself up with an unrealistic expectation if you try to have a perfect relationship. A figure skater can score a ten. A student may get a perfect score of 2400 on his SAT. **But no one ever achieves perfection in relationships.**

Instead of striving to have a perfect relationship, I would love to see couples strive to have more "human" or genuine relations. Now it may sound absurd to you that I would recommend we strive to be more human, but it's not. Many problems in life are caused by a denial of our humanity. We try to be more than human. We act as though being ourselves isn't enough and therefore we have to be more than ourselves—we must be perfect!

We are the only species on this planet that tries to be something we are not. You don't see an elephant wanting to be a giraffe. They are what they are. But we are driven to be different than we are. When we endeavor to have a perfect relationship, we are courting disaster. Eventually the relationship is going to suffer.

Our striving for perfect romance, perfect security and perfect prestige is motivated by emotional dependency. From this dependency stem demands—demands on our partner to be perfect, to be the way we need them to be in order for us to feel good about ourselves. This pressure—sometimes overt, sometimes covert—creates all sorts of problems in our relationships.

The couple celebrating their fiftieth wedding anniversary had come for counseling in their forty-eighth year together. Wow. What an incredible statement of their commitment. No one has a perfect partner or a perfect relationship. All marriages are works in process. The point is that if we are willing to grow along these lines, we will become the best partner we can possibly be.

A GOOD RELATIONSHIP IS
BASED ON COMPROMISE.

THE REALITY: Compromise has been confused with submission. Submitting to your partner's desires will breed resentment and retaliation, not harmony.

Consider two scenarios:

1. Peter was married to an extremely angry, volatile woman and was being controlled by his wife's explosive personality. He constantly strove to keep Mary from becoming upset. One Sunday, Peter agreed to go to the grocery store with Mary to pick up a couple of items for dinner. He counted on getting in and out of the store as quickly as possible. However, Mary decided to turn the errand into a major shopping trip. When she pulled out coupon books and began adding items to the list, Peter expressed his objection to the change in plans.

Mary blew up. "All you ever do is think about yourself," she said.

Rather than escalate the conflict, Peter backed down, saying, "Okay. I'll take you shopping." But after giving in to make peace, Peter felt terrible. He resented Mary for manipulating him and sulked the rest of the day.

2. Jamie wanted his wife, Carol, to go skiing, but she had no interest in the sport. Jamie was really disappointed and said so,

but he respected Carol's position and didn't try to convince her to do what he wanted. Instead they discussed Jamie's frustration and teased out its two components: He wanted to go skiing, and he wanted to spend time with Carol. Both were important to him. Carol searched her desires and said she wanted to spend time with Jamie, but that while it would be nice to have a weekend away, she was worried about grading the exams of her freshman chemistry class. Together they worked out a plan. They decided to go to the mountains and while Jamie skis, Carol would grade the exams and take a nature hike and together they would—well, you can use your imagination.

Jamie and Carol's solution represents a genuine compromise, but the situation in scenario one is riddled with submission. Peter believed he was compromising to make peace when he agreed to take Mary shopping, but he wasn't. He was capitulating to Mary's emotional blackmail. He was losing himself in the relationship because he was emotionally dependent on her.

Our strong desire to please our partner creates an attitude that suggests we should minimize interpersonal conflict. One way of avoiding clashes is to comply with the aggressive partner's demands. This is a common, but unhealthy, practice. **Submission breeds resentment, and oppression ensures retaliation.**

The problem is that **most couples are confused about the difference between submission and compromise.** Most of the patients I've confronted about being too acquiescent exclaim, "I'm only trying to compromise. Isn't that what you have to do to make a relationship work?"

The notion that a good relationship is based on giving in is actually destructive. When we yield to another person's desires without really wanting to, we will eventually make them pay a price for our compliance, one way or another, consciously or unconsciously.

Remember, a true compromise is only achieved when both parties walk away from the negotiating table as winners.

WE NEED TO WORK HARDER AT OUR RELATIONSHIP.

THE REALITY: More effort in a troubled relationship rarely produces positive results. What is needed is new information, not more effort.

Working harder at a relationship is usually a waste of time. Many couples experiencing discord promise each other to work harder on the relationship, and they actually do. Then they are bewildered that after a period of honest, sustained effort, all their misery is still intact. **Working harder at a relationship is not effective because the only efforts someone can undertake are what he or she already knows how to do.**

Denise knew how important it was to share honest feelings with her partner. She'd grown up in a silent household riddled with subterranean resentments and discounted feelings. She vowed she would never be caught in such a marriage, yet she wed Eric, a quiet, intense man not unlike her father.

Eric was pleasant but distant, and Denise's requests for more intimacy made him uncomfortable. Denise persisted in expressing her feelings of hurt and disappointment, hoping that her openness would encourage Eric to discuss his feelings. Instead he withdrew even more.

I liken Denise to an amateur cook who makes exquisite lemon pies crested with lightly toasted meringue. Constantly praised by family members and friends, the cook (who now likes to be called a chef) opens a sidewalk cafe with marine blue awnings and begins turning out scrumptious lemon meringue pies. However, despite the perfect pies, the restaurant quickly closes. The chef did not know how to make anything else.

To improve romantic relationships, we first use all skills currently available, as Denise did, but when problems continue, we need to expand our repertoire. We must get a new recipe. **New information, not more effort, is what we need.** What Denise finally learned to do was to meet Eric where he was, rather than try to take Eric to where she was. In therapy she talked with Eric about his silence, and he began to tell her what his silence was really saying. I remember a very powerful session in which Eric turned to Denise with tears in his eyes and said, "There is so much love that I have inside of me for you, but it is blocked. I feel like there is a cork stuck in my throat, and no matter what I do to uncork it, it remains. I do want you to feel my love for you, but I am stuck." This was a very critical moment in the couple's therapy. Hopefully, you will learn how to create these special moments in your relationship with some of the recipes included in this book.

DESIRE EQUALS ABILITY.

THE REALITY: Our emotional desire to be a good partner exceeds our ability.

We Americans live in a can-do society. We have an enormous amount of faith in our ability to solve problems, and we are very reluctant to accept personal limitations. Most of us believe that if we have the desire to make a relationship work, we should be able to do it. This isn't true! **Keeping a relationship going requires a particular set of skills, like holding on to your self *and* a strong desire or commitment. Desire alone, however, is not enough.**

An analogy that I often use to illustrate this idea is my love for tennis. I would love to win the Wimbledon tennis championship. My desire and my love for the game rival that of any professional tennis player. If you don't believe me, just ask my dear friend, Roger. However, even during my most grandiose moments, I cannot escape from the fact that I simply do not possess the athletic abilities and tennis skills necessary to become a champion of this caliber. I've the heart, but not the strokes.

None of us comes equipped with all of the skills we will need throughout the life of a long-term relationship. We must learn through our mistakes, through reading articles and books on intimate relationships, attending lectures and seminars, discussing our situations with trusted friends, grinding with our partner, and sometimes seeking professional help.

Think of yourself as an athlete training for a marathon. Only conscious effort will enable you to go the distance and reap the joy of a loving partnership. Use your desire to help you find the path that will increase your ability to couple. In chapter 5 we will explore the three skills that I consider mandatory for maintaining a healthy relationship: (1) Saying what you like and don't like, (2) negotiating differences from a position of respect for your mate, and (3) striving for mutually satisfying solutions. Without these skills it will be extremely hard to have a fulfilling relationship, no matter how strong your motivation is. Desire is only one of the ingredients needed for success.

MYTH 10:

TILL DEATH DO US PART!

THE REALITY: Romantic relationships and marriages are held together with an extremely fragile emotional bond. Taking a relationship for granted is dangerous and will often result in tragedy.

Clichéd Westerns always ended with a cowboy and heroine riding off into a glorious sunset, a metaphor for their rosy future. Even today many of us continue to enter relationships with the belief that we have a lifelong commitment from our mate, especially if we marry.

However, the reality is that all romantic relationships have a "'fragile bond" that must be nurtured. I've seen hundreds of men and women who, after years of ignoring the quality of their relationships, express shock when a partner decides to leave. They'd based their entire future on the myth that marriage involves a lifelong commitment.

Ed and Louise came for marriage counseling after nineteen years together. Their son and daughter had entered college, and Louise announced that she wanted a divorce. Ed was absolutely stunned and managed to persuade Louise to see me in a last-ditch effort, but Louise's love had died long ago. Over the years Ed had brushed aside all of her efforts to revitalize the marriage, and Louise no longer wished to be with him.

I tell couples that their first child is their relationship. When two people come together, a third entity is created that needs as much care and attention as a human infant. With proper nourishment, the relationship will thrive. Without it, a slow death will inevitably occur. This is what happened to Ed and Louise. Ed was devastated for over a year after Louise divorced him. But he learned a very important lesson: Never take your relationship for granted.

Effort, attention and a constant flow of new information can all help make a relationship mutually satisfying, but even these offer no guarantee. The only assurance I can give you is that no one readily gives up a good thing, and your chances for longevity improve when both partners make the union a priority and wholeheartedly strive to create a mutually satisfying relationship.

CHAPTER 3

Seven Deadly Expectations in Relationships

One of the oddest features of Western Christianized culture is its ready acceptance of the myth of the stable family and the happy marriage. We have been taught to accept the myth not as an heroic ideal, something good, brave, and nearly impossible to fulfill, but as the very fiber of normal life. Given most families and most marriages, the belief seems not admirable but foolhardy.

—JONATHAN RABAN (1987)

43

Unconditional Love

Probably the most persistent and dangerous expectation we have is the notion that we will give and receive love with no expectations. Even after forty years, the human potential movement of the 1960s exerts an incredible influence on everyone living in this culture—those who lived through that social revolution and those born in its aftermath.

Through weekend marathons and sensitivity training seminars, we learned a whole new way of talking to each other. We were encouraged to make "I" statements. We probed our feelings, were rebirthed, yelled at empty chairs to resolve unfinished business and confronted our "shadows" in an unending quest for personal growth and development.

The movement also created a blueprint for relationships that continues to influence our notions of ideal romantic relationships. Its central concept of unconditional love was infinitely comforting after the restrictive values and expectations of the 1950s. Many of us enthusiastically and naively embraced these revolutionary ideas and entered relationships based on the credo of unconditional love. Yet, even the most determined of us continued to have expectations. We just didn't express them to our partners. The inevitable and painful outcome is that many of us have stewed unhappily in silence, feeling guilty or ashamed that we have expectations of our partners.

The truth is we all have expectations. Expectations are naturally generated by our brains and therefore are inevitable in relationships. But there are two kinds: those we can refer to as "reasonable" and those that are "unreasonable." By reasonable I mean those ideas, perceptions or expectations that are reality-based. Reasonable expectations facilitate intimacy, togetherness, cooperation and teamwork. Unreasonable expectations, on the other hand, are based not on reality but on some ideal or fantasy of how things should be.

Unreasonable expectations obstruct intimacy and impair our ability to hold on to ourselves while we stay connected with our partners and see our partners as they truly are.

The enormous popularity of self-help books and seminars led by educators such as Stephen Covey and provocative media therapists like Dr. Laura Schlessinger and Dr. Phil reflects a willingness to become more honest with our selves and learn about how to cope with relationships. Hopefully, we are learning that striving for perfection is futile and realizing that our most important goal is to become more human. Accepting that we have expectations and being willing to challenge our own expectations is an important step on this journey.

Unreasonable Expectations

I once had a patient named Madelyn tell me that her husband was extremely critical. She recalled the following example as proof. After spending a near-perfect day together walking some beautiful mountain trails, she decided to prepare her husband's favorite meal, Louisiana gumbo. She knew Jake loved to eat cornbread muffins with his gumbo, so she prepared a batch from scratch. As they were eating, Jake complimented her on cooking a "mighty fine gumbo" and added that next time he'd like for her to take the muffins from the oven before the bottoms became crisp. Madelyn was so deeply offended by his request that when

Jake asked how he could have conveyed the information without hurting her feelings, she refused to answer. She felt he was inconsiderate and ungrateful to make such a remark after she'd worked so hard on the meal.

So what do you think about Madelyn's position? Is her expectation reasonable or unreasonable? In my opinion, she was clearly unreasonable. How is she going to know what he wants, unless he tells her? Sure, his timing may have been poor, but the point is that in order for Madelyn and Jake to learn how to cooperate and please each other they need to welcome opportunities to learn about each other and not tag these disclosures with silence-inducing labels such as "inconsiderate" or "ungrateful." When I described to Madelyn the catch-22 she was placing Jake in, she was truly surprised. She'd thought that her expectation was quite reasonable.

I'm sure that, if asked, every one of us would say our expectations are reasonable. However, we have all experienced moments of clarity when we've caught a glimpse of our own unreasonableness.

I confess that many of my own expectations have been outrageous. A situation from my first marriage provides a poignant example. My first wife was a childhood sweetheart. We met in Chicago when I was working at Mailings, a woman's shoe store—not the most romantic beginning—but our youth and innocence made up for that. We dated for about a year and then I joined the Marine Corps. I served for three years, a period that changed my life.

While I was in the Marine Corps, I discovered my interest in psychology and counseling. I was honorably discharged in 1972 and subsequently I began my college education. I was constantly seeking to become a better therapist, and in 1974 I attended the annual meeting of the Association of Humanistic Psychology in Chicago. I decided to look up Denise and talk about old times. We met and discovered we were still in love.

Our courtship was intense, and within six months we moved in together and began planning our wedding. We were both attending college, but beyond our immediate educational goals, we were very vague about what we wanted. As our marriage matured and deepened, I realized that I wanted to have children. We had spoken of children briefly before getting married, and I recall Denise being unsure about how she felt about having children. I naively believed that one day she would change her mind. Well, she didn't. She became more and more certain that she didn't want children, whereas my desire to be a father increased.

I'm ashamed at how I handled myself at this point in the relationship. I tried everything to get Denise to change her mind. I accused her of not being a "real woman." We had terrible fights, and I was very cruel because I didn't know how to discuss my disappointment over her decision. I loved her, but I also wanted to be a father. Now here's where I was incredibly outrageous: I expected her to honor my needs instead of her own.

At the time I felt justified in my expectation. I would declare that what I wanted was "normal." To deceive myself and manipulate her, I argued my expectations were "reasonable" and "fair." How dare she think otherwise! In fact, as I became more honest with myself, I realized that this was a typical ploy on my part. I accused anyone opposed to me of being unreasonable.

Actually, I wasn't interested in being fair. I wanted things to go my way! I was unreasonable! And I confess that I still am. The first time I recognized my unreasonableness, I felt ashamed but, at the same time, liberated.

Today, I realize that **we all want things to go our way,** and that's no crime, especially if we are honest with ourselves and our partners. I've also discovered a paradox: I am a lot more reasonable after being honest about how unreasonable I am. Isn't that strange?

Let's examine seven unreasonable expectations that people typically think are reasonable.

WE ARE ADULTS AND THEREFORE SHOULD BE ABLE TO COMMUNICATE LIKE ADULTS AND TELL EACH OTHER WHAT WE LIKE AND DON'T LIKE.

THE REALITY: We have a difficult time telling each other what we like and don't like, especially when it comes to more personal issues.

We are all rather eloquent when it comes to talking about city council elections, the Super Bowl or our neighbors' loud parties, but we become almost mute when we try to express ourselves on an intimate level. We are surprised when the most articulate person has trouble being personal. Why? Because we confuse adulthood with being mature. Because we are adults, we assume that we should be able to discuss our innermost feelings and desires. But we can't! **Partners do not readily tell each other what they**

like and don't like. In fact, a realistic view is to anticipate that you and your partner will have difficulty communicating intimate thoughts to each other—especially as you become increasingly important to each other.

So why don't people who love each other communicate their most important and intimate desires and feelings? Is it that we just don't care? I think not. It's really the opposite problem. It's because you are too important to each other.

We are too concerned with what our partners have to say to us, so we avoid discussions of difficult personal issues. When a person becomes too important to us, it means that our ability to hold on to ourselves is not equal to the degree of importance the person has acquired in our lives. This is called emotional dependency. When we are emotionally dependent upon a person, we dare not share an important or controversial feeling or thought for fear of what might happen between us. We make our partners too important, and therefore we either just give in to the connection, try to control them or withdraw.

If you have the ability to hold on to your self, you will be able to respond appropriately to whatever your partner has to say. You will set appropriate boundaries and appropriately assert yourself if necessary. You will be able to stay balanced regardless of his or her position.

Personal Language

Personal language is a unique form of communication. It is different from social language, which is rooted in the types of communication used to navigate a transaction such as a bank loan.

The goal of personal language is very different. The goal of personal language is to hold on to your self as you remain connected to your partner. Setting boundaries is the way we hold on to ourselves in relationships. There are three types of boundaries that we set with our personal language: (1) What is okay and not okay for others to do with us, (2) what is okay and not okay for us to do in our relationships, and (3) who we are—what is important to us, what we want and like, and what we don't want and don't like. Personal language helps us define, manage and respect our boundaries.

Let's take a closer look at how we develop our personal language. First, in order for me to be able to talk with you about what I want, I need to have an idea about what is important to me. **Self-awareness is a cornerstone of personal language.**

A solid sense of self develops from childhood experiences. When we asked our parents to watch us while we were swinging at the park, we were asking for our parents to see us or recognize us. We wanted them to recognize our feelings, to mirror our excitement and joy. Empathic responses like, "You're really having fun on the swing," or, "You're really proud of yourself, swinging so high," help a child develop a sense of self. An empathic response holds a mirror up to a child and offers an opportunity for the child to see herself or himself through the eyes of the parent.

Unfortunately, instead of seeing us as we were, our parents were too busy trying to be positive or dealing with their own anxiety. Go to any park where children are playing on a Sunday afternoon and statements like "That's good!" or "I really like that!" or "Be careful, you might hurt yourself" will be heard echoing throughout the park. These parents don't realize it, but they are giving their children the wrong message.

I imagine that some of you are saying, "I read that positive feedback would improve my child's self-esteem." It's not true! We have been led astray by the well-intentioned psychologists who recommend this procedure.

How can positive feedback damage a child? When parents reward a child's experience with positive feedback, the child's attention shifts away from what he or she is feeling about his or her own behavior to what the parents are feeling. This shift in focus interferes with the development of a sense of self. The child focuses on what is important to the parent, instead of what is important to the child. If this pattern persists, the child's motivation will switch from doing things that are intrinsically rewarding to doing things that please others. This is a subtle but deadly shift in a child's psychological development. Unfortunately, it is a wound that most of us can relate to.

Those among us fortunate enough to receive empathetic responses from our parents will have developed a sense of who we are and what is important to us. But knowing what you want is just half of the solution. You also need to feel worthy of asking for what you want. Therefore, self-worth is the second essential in personal language.

Self-esteem is influenced by how our parents responded to us and to our needs. Did they respect us when we said, "No"? Did they show an interest in our needs? Were we encouraged to say what we wanted? Did they celebrate our existence, or were we burdens?

It's tragic, but true, that there are people who have never heard a message from their parents like "I'm glad you are my son," or "I'm proud of you," or "I have confidence in you," or "I am interested in what you have to say!" The emotional climate in a family influences the development of the self-worth we must have in order to develop the personal language we need to express and struggle for our personal desires.

Sometimes the first step to helping a patient deal with low self-esteem is to ask him or her to declare their feelings of unworthiness. Two years ago, a young couple came to me for counseling because their nine-month-old marriage seemed like a mistake. "We never have fun anymore," Jeff said. "We go to a concert and she looks bored. We go out to eat and she looks like she has indigestion. Not to mention sex. You can just imagine that."

"I don't know why you're blaming me," Phyllis said. "I go along with all your plans. Look at me—I'm sitting here in a shrink's office right this minute."

"You never said you didn't want to come here," Jeff stammered, looking surprised. They were both emotionally dependent. They were emotionally fused, which meant that almost everything that occurred between them was taken personally.

Phyllis had, in fact, diagnosed what was wrong with their relationship. She had abandoned her self when she and Jeff got married and simply went along with whatever Jeff put forward. However, her suppressed anger drained all joy from the marriage and left Phyllis depressed. Jeff, on the other hand, was too focused on how Phyllis was feeling. He didn't know how to keep centered, regardless of what Phyllis was feeling or doing.

Fortunately, they decided to continue therapy. Phyllis started taking risks and expressing her likes and dislikes to Jeff, but it was slow going. Often she truly didn't know what she wanted.

Then one week Phyllis came in excited. She related to me an incident in which she glimpsed the process she was caught in. Jeff had asked her if she wished to go out for Chinese or Mexican food.

She'd shrugged and said it didn't matter. But as soon as she entered the Chinese restaurant, she immediately imagined wonderful cheese enchiladas and realized that secretly she'd been hoping Jeff would choose the Mexican food. She turned to Jeff and said, "I've changed my mind. I'd rather go to the Mexican restaurant."

She had discovered the pattern that dominated her life and started to change it by asking Jeff for what she wanted. Phyllis's inability to express her desires affected every important aspect of the young marriage: saving for a down payment on a house, family planning, deciding where to celebrate religious holidays.

Her low self-worth kept her from comfortably stating her preferences. In therapy, she discovered that she had both a right and a responsibility to tell Jeff her true desires and perceptions. **When you withhold your true desires from your partner, you are literally abandoning yourself. If you want to be a good partner and have a satisfying relationship, you need to learn how to communicate your personal desires to your partner.**

We often act like Phyllis even though we **do** know our desires. We are simply afraid to tell our partner what we really think or feel because we sense they don't want to hear it. Dr. David Schnarch noted in his outstanding book, *Passionate Marriage*, that on entering a restaurant, you can immediately distinguish the longtime couples from couples who are dating. The two people dating are talking to each other while the long-time couples are sitting silently—and not because there is nothing to say. There are plenty of things they need to say to each other, but they don't dare address them.

Most of us withhold our personal desires because we're worried about how our partners will respond. We are emotionally dependent, and therefore we don't follow our own directives. We either submit to our partner's will or withdraw. In essence we are making our behavior contingent upon how our partners will respond.

Another reason we withhold our desires is because we have never learned how to discuss personal matters. Most of our parents protected us from parental discord, and so we've never seen adults hash out their issues in a healthy way (although some of us have witnessed ugly confrontations).

When we start expressing our own needs, we will worry more about what we need to say or who we want to be than our partner's reactions. We say what we need to say to honor our integrity. **In a healthy relationship, you keep in touch with your personal desires and you stay connected to your partner.**

As a result, most of us simply don't have the skill to discuss, in a friendly manner, what we don't like. Here is an example. Let's say that for some reason, incomprehensible to you, your partner suddenly begins calling you "Cuddles." You realize this is intended as an endearment, so you say nothing. Yet, as time passes, you hate "Cuddles" more and more. It's a name for a puppy or an infant. Besides, you like your own name just fine.

At last when your partner introduces you to a coworker at the company Christmas party as "Cuddles", you lose it. "Stop calling me that!" you hiss and storm off to take up a vigil beside the punch bowl for the remainder of the evening. In the car on the way home you enlighten your partner about a whole list of behaviors you abhor: leaving the garden hose uncoiled; incurring late fees on mortgage payments; always arriving at least ten minutes late. You are amazed to find that you are shaking with rage.

If you were able to speak up for yourself when he first called you "Cuddles", you would have discussed and hopefully resolved the issue, and you wouldn't have needed to blow up.

Talking to each other personally requires taking a risk and delivering your whole message, not just part of it. Remember that asking for what you want does not mean that you will get it, or even get an empathetic response. Don't approach this task expecting your partner to respond positively. If you do, you are going to be disappointed. Instead, base your motivation for communicating openly on your desire to act with integrity. You and you alone have the ability to keep your integrity in your relationship. Integrity allows you to both join in the relationship and honor your individuality.

By now it should be clear that it is unreasonable to expect that you and your partner will be able to communicate with each other on a personal, intimate level. Therefore, **when you run into this difficulty, your first response should be, "Of course we are having trouble discussing our personal desires with each other. It's to be expected."**

UNDERSTANDING EACH OTHER IS EASY.

THE REALITY: Nothing could be further from the truth. Understanding each other is nearly impossible in a relationship.

Since understanding each other depends a great deal on direct communication, it's highly unlikely we will achieve a deep understanding with a partner if we can't authentically and honestly discuss what is important to us. However, our communication difficulty is only part of the problem.

Every relationship is what I would refer to as a mixed marriage. We tend to think of mixed marriages only in terms of ethnicity or religion: black and white; Catholic and Jew. But this view is too narrow. Even if partners share the same religious beliefs or are the same color, they are still in a mixed marriage because **every one of us was raised in a unique subculture.** Each family in this society creates a unique worldview with a set of rules and expectations that filter and define your experiences. You learn what love is, how to deal with disappointment, how to get what you want, how to divide household responsibilities, and the appropriate roles for men and women in a relationship.

What you learned in your family is normal for you. This is your baseline. It forms and shapes your expectations. But what's normal for you may be completely alien to your partner. Therefore, true understanding is something that must be sought and cultivated.

When Claudia and Roger came for their first appointment with me, Claudia haltingly described the crisis in their relationship. Her eyes filled with tears as she told me, "It just feels like he doesn't love me. He yells at me all the time."

As I explored Claudia's background, I discovered that in her family, thoughts, ideas and feelings were expressed matter-of-factly, in a very low tone of voice. Everyone in her family spoke calmly and reasonably, even when they were upset or passionate. A raised voice signified an immensely serious problem.

Roger's background was quite different. He'd grown up in an Italian American family where people measured love by the degree of involvement and engagement they experienced with each other. Fiery, passionate speech, even yelling, meant that you were interested in the person you were talking to. Therefore, what for Roger was "loving behavior" signaled a lack of love to Claudia. Eventually, Claudia and Roger came to realize that the dramatic difference in their backgrounds created most of the misunderstandings in their marriage.

At first the idea of cultivating a relationship may seem unattractive because we've been told that a "good relationship" flows naturally without any work on our parts, just as our hearts beat without any conscious effort. Nothing could be further from the truth. Don't blindly accept this idea because if you do, you may walk away from a relationship that could be good for you if you're willing to put some effort into establishing a mutual understanding.

IF YOU LOVE SOMEONE, YOU WILL RESPECT THE PERSON'S DIFFERENCES.

THE REALITY: The exact opposite is true. Most couples have tremendous difficulty respecting each other's differences.

Our misunderstandings and poorly developed personal language make respect a formidable task. Let's examine this from several different angles.

Most of us have not grown up in families in which respect for differences was nourished. It's more likely that differences were tagged as disloyal, stupid or problematic with cutting remarks such as, "How could you make such a stupid decision?" Even those of us who didn't hear such comments probably picked up on disapproving attitudes.

We try to cope with our inability to respect differences by creating the illusion that we don't have differences with the one we love. But we do.

➠ Because I have a strong need to be on time, I assume that you do too. But, in fact, your style is "laid back," and you resent being hurried as much as I hate being late.

➠ My energy level is highest in the morning, and when there's a household project to be completed such as cleaning out the garage, I expect you to get up early on Saturday to tackle the job with me. I may accuse you of being lazy when you won't. You, on the other hand, are more energetic at night and may begin calculating the income tax return long after I've gone to bed.

➠ I grew up in a family where open displays of affection were rare, so I am embarrassed when you fling your arms around me while we stand on a street corner waiting for the traffic light to change. I consider even holding hands in public indiscreet. I'd rather demonstrate affection other ways. I might surprise you with a CD you've been wanting or drive the carpool for you.

The list could go on and on. Let me share a personal example. By the time my second wife, Dymph, and I had been married for two years, I had become extremely annoyed with her desire for small talk. Although I did not verbalize my frustration, my attitude was communicating something like, "Don't bother me with small talk. YOU ARE DISTRACTING ME."

Then one evening she began discussing her feelings about our pending decision to buy a condominium we had been looking at. She mentioned that it faced west rather then east, that it was on the second floor rather than the first, that it had sunlight. After listening for what seemed hours, I impatiently said, "Just tell me whether or not you want to buy the condominium."

She said, "I'm not sure yet. I just need to talk with you more about it before I make a decision." This baffled me. I found conversation distracting. How could it help her clarify what she wanted to do? I went away from this interaction shaking my head. How could we be so different?

The next week I told my dear friend Dr. Kempler that I knew something wasn't right about how I was treating Dymph, but I wasn't sure what it was. He pointed out that Dymph and I are very different. I need silence to discover my true feelings, while Dymph finds herself through conversation. Talking about what was going on helped her find her position on any given issue. For me, talking was a distraction.

Our friend's analysis provided extremely valuable insight into our difficulty. It opened up a whole new way of understanding this struggle in our relationship. The result was that I became a bit better at respecting Dymph's need for conversation, and she became better at understanding my need for silence.

Neither approach was better than the other, only different. Sometimes when you are struggling with your differences, stop and ask yourself, "Do I want to be right or happy?" When we understand that our partner's differences are natural and worthy, we deepen our connection and strengthen the relationship.

Respect is a two-way street. In counseling couples where lack of respect is an issue, I've found both parties equally at fault. The person who complains about a lack of respect usually responds incredulously to this idea. "What do you mean? I'm not the abusive one, he is."

The person protesting his or her innocence is usually unaware that he or she also acts disrespectfully. Often family therapists can help clients see that the dynamics in a relationship are opposite to what they appear to be. The person victimized will become the persecutor.

Realizing that respect is a reciprocal process may help you see what you can do to address this problem in your relationship. Here is my suggestion: Take an honest look at your behavior. I guarantee that if you are rigorously honest with yourself you will discover that you are disrespectful too. You can't change how your partner behaves, but you can clean up your side of the street. Your best chance to create more respect in your relationship is to start addressing your behavior first. Forget about focusing on what your partner is doing. Let the best of you do the thinking and speaking when you hit rough spots. You'll be pleasantly surprised with the results.

UNREASONABLE EXPECTATION 4:

A GOOD RELATIONSHIP IS BASED ON TRUST.

THE REALITY: We trust each other much more than we should. True trust needs to be grounded in the reality of who each of us are and not on some ideal of how we should feel in a relationship.

You can go to the self-help section of a bookstore and choose any book on relationships and find a chapter espousing the values and virtues of trust. We talk about trust so glibly that it creates the illusion that something is terribly wrong if you don't have complete trust from your partner. This is utter nonsense.

By now you must realize that a person who can't express himself or herself on a personal level and has trouble respecting differences is a person who can't be trusted. It is naïve to trust someone who is unable to express what he or she needs.

But that's not the only reason we should be more circumspect with our trust. Here is the other part of the story. **Today, trust is falsely based on the notion that our partners will take better care of us than we take of ourselves.**

People who rely on others to take better care of them than they do describe themselves as "trusting." The reality is that they are not trusting; they are naïve! **Trust cannot be created by only looking outward.** A person who is focused solely on what his partner is or is not doing ignores all of the information that he would have if he were also paying attention to himself. We must heed the advice of William Shakespeare:

> *To thine own self be true.*
> *And it must follow, as the night, the day.*
> *Thou canst not then be false to any man.*

Trusting yourself to react according to what you perceive is indispensable in forming a climate of trust. The most critical contribution you can make in developing a trusting atmosphere in your relationship is to respond to what you perceive. When you ignore your gut feelings, or when you minimize your distress, you are betraying yourself and setting yourself up to become a victim. I've talked with literally hundreds of betrayed partners who continued to trust an untrustworthy partner, even though they intuitively knew they shouldn't.

Stan and Cathy came to see me in a severe crisis. Stan was having another affair, and Cathy was threatening suicide. They'd been married for five years, and this was Stan's third affair.

The pattern for all three affairs was similar. Stan would feel upset with some aspect of the marriage, such as Cathy's weight gain, but he wouldn't talk with Cathy about his dissatisfaction. Instead he would begin staying out late with friends at a pool hall. He was a good-looking man, and eventually a woman would approach him and he would become romantically involved with her.

After about a month of acting differently, Cathy would confront him, but Stan would deny he was having an affair so vigorously that Cathy would begin to question her sanity. However, her suspicions would continue until she'd shift into a Sherlock Holmes mode, eventually catching Stan in a lie or surreptitiously following him to the bar and seeing him with the other woman.

Then she'd launch into an emotional barrage, shaming Stan for his dishonesty, betrayal and lack of concern. Stan's guilt would generate severe remorse and promises to never hurt Cathy again—and Cathy would believe him. For a short while the relationship would improve, but inevitably, the couple would return to their old behavior and the negative cycle would begin once more.

Many of us are like Cathy. We've come to believe that if we love someone, we must show trust in our partners even if they don't deserve it. This is a very gullible way of functioning in the world and will invariably result in many sorrowful and disillusioning experiences. Cathy had no reason to trust Stan when he swore, "I will never have another affair again." The only way that Cathy could develop trust in her relationship with Stan would be to address the serious problems in their marriage.

The affairs were the smoke, not the fire. Stan wanted marriage to be easy and was unable to struggle for what he wanted. He didn't know how to discuss what he wanted from Cathy, and after some therapy he realized that he had also feared becoming dependent upon her. Cathy, on the other hand, needed to learn to rely on her feelings more, to stay centered and to be more appropriately assertive.

When I told Cathy that she needed to openly distrust her husband, she was initially confused, but relieved. A first step to repairing betrayal in this marriage was to have Stan encourage Cathy to openly doubt him. Because Stan was committed to the relationship, he was able to give Cathy the authority to openly distrust him and take whatever measures she needed to ensure she was not being deceived again.

Eventually Cathy learned to have faith in Stan. Faith is unrelated to trust. Faith is grounded in the knowledge that every person has an intrinsic motivation for learning. Every person has a desire to become a more complete person and make the best possible adaptation to life given the set of circumstances he or she perceives. This is a psychological law of nature.

You can place your faith in the awareness that these forces are operating in your partner. He or she is learning from experience, often not as fast as you or I would like them to, but nonetheless they are acquiring information. Base your faith on this.

Am I trustworthy?

Another responsibility we often ignore is asking ourselves whether we are trustworthy. **We must ask ourselves, "Am I part of the trust/mistrust problem?"** The answer is always and emphatically "Yes!" For instance, if someone is lying to me, upon reflection I am likely to discover that by my past reactions, I am making it hard for him or her to be honest. If my partner doesn't confront me with her unhappiness, it may be because I am presenting myself as so fragile that I am implicitly telling her that I must be protected from the truth. **I believe that if we are honest with ourselves, we all will realize that we fall short of holding up our end of the bargain.**

I want you to feel empowered in your relationships, relying on yourself to respond and react according to what you sense is essential to a foundation of trust. **Being a good partner does** not mean shielding your mate from reality. It means that you help your partner face reality with you at his or her side. We will all be better partners if we have more faith and less trust in our partners.

SINCE WE ARE ADULTS, WE SHOULD BE ABLE TO DISCUSS AND NEGOTIATE OUR DIFFERENCES.

THE REALITY: Few of us know how to negotiate in a mutually satisfying way. We are stuck in a win/lose drama in which we either relentlessly strive to stay on the winning end of the proposition or resign and become the perennial losers.

"Lucy, let's sit down and talk this over like adults." Two generations of television viewers have heard Desi Arnaz make this suggestion to Lucille Ball with disastrous results. Remember the commotion that always ensued when those two sat down to work on a problem?

I think their TV scenes are actually pretty realistic. Most of us are not much more effective than Lucy and Ricky in problem-solving, although we're probably less rowdy. Being an adult doesn't automatically confer negotiating skills. The sooner you admit your ignorance, the sooner you can learn how to negotiate.

At the heart of a successful negotiation lies the "quid pro quo," a "something for something" agreement. Most couples resist approaching their relationship from this businesslike perspective because, they argue, "It takes the romance out of the relationship." I am convinced that learning how to come to terms with your partner is a critical skill in developing a healthy relationship. It won't remove romance from your relationship. In fact, it will produce less conflict and tension and create more room for romance.

Sam and Naomi came to counseling because of their incessant bickering. Every attempt to debate an issue resulted in an endless, draining struggle. Wrangling also contaminated their negotiations. I remember one session in which they were talking about where to live after retirement, which was two years away.

Naomi suggested the mountains. Everything about mountain life appealed to her: fresh air, natural beauty, lack of crowds. Sam hated the mountains and immediately launched into a tirade, attacking Naomi's character. "All you ever think about is what you want. I've worked hard all my life to support you, and you still don't appreciate what I have done for you. The mountains would be the worst place for me to live with my arthritis." Sam preferred a location with a warm, dry climate year-round like Phoenix or Las Vegas.

I listened patiently for about five minutes and then I confronted each of them for how rotten they were treating each other. I suggested that they had never learned how to be partners. I asked them if they would continue to explore the retirement issue with the following perspective in mind: "Treat your needs and your partner's needs with equal importance, and feel free to negotiate with your partner by offering him or her something in order to meet your own goal."

The effect was remarkable. Sam and Naomi suddenly began to work together as a team and finally decided to establish two residences, one in the California Sierras and one in Las Vegas. Sam offered to spend the summers in the mountains if Naomi would spend the winters in Las Vegas. She was hesitant at first, but she realized that this was a "something for something" agreement, an agreement that would give each of them some of what they wanted. For the first time in their marriage, they joined forces and functioned as partners rather than moving against one another as enemies.

When a negotiation is successful, everyone involved will feel that his or her needs were recognized, respected and satisfied. The solution will be a synthesis of what everyone wants. Everyone wins!

UNREASONABLE EXPECTATION 6:

WE KNOW HOW TO FUNCTION IN A RELATIONSHIP.

THE REALITY: We are all ignorant and incompetent in relationship matters.

By now it should be clear that not only is it unrealistic, but absurd, to expect that we should know how to function well in a relationship. If you accept what I have said so far, then you must see that you are ignorant when it comes to having a healthy relationship.

I can understand if you feel discouraged at this point. This is a pretty dismal admission, isn't it? When I reach this point in a workshop, I often mention that this talk is sponsored by Eli Lilly and Company, the pharmaceutical manufacturer that produces Prozac, an antidepressant. And yet, paradoxically, many men and women have found this realization to be their only hope in reconciling a bad relationship!

Why does this type of admission help? It helps because humility is liberating, and there is no larger chunk of humble pie to swallow than acknowledging this shortcoming. Accepting one's limitations is an important step in establishing a climate within our lives and our relationships for growth and enrichment.

By letting go of our facades and charades, we make possible a reality-based relationship in which mistakes are expected and welcomed because they carry important information. When we have successfully created such an atmosphere, we will begin to have a relationship that is based on the reality of who we are, rather than on illusions created by fantasy, and unrealistic and unreasonable expectations. We will stop acting as if we know how to have a relationship and start the journey of self-discovery that will lead to emotional maturity, a journey that can only be fueled by honesty, willingness and humility.

It's not uncommon for us to idealize a person we love. When we do, we fail to recognize that our partners know no more about how to function in a relationship than we do. It's a fact that we marry a person whose level of emotional maturity is similar to our own. When we ignore this fact, we end up expecting our partner to be more than they are. Lovers desire to please and will try to oblige us.

The result is that most of us try to be more than we are in our relationships. The fear that usually motivates this kind of behavior is "You will not love me unless I'm what you want, or at least real close to it."

A young couple who had been bitterly fighting for the better part of their marriage came to see me in hopes of stopping their incessant arguing. Here's how they presented their problem.

Alice wanted more time and attention from Fred. She complained that Fred worked too much and that when she tried to talk with him he would get angry. (Time is often mistakenly identified as a problem between partners. It is never the real issue. The real issue is related to the quality of their connection.)

Fred stated that he had tried to accommodate Alice by coming home earlier, but Alice still complained and criticized him. This led Fred to conclude that Alice couldn't be satisfied. (In a way, Fred's diagnosis was correct. Alice was insatiable because she was asking for the wrong thing from Fred. What Alice really wanted was a better connection.)

Fred didn't know how to hold on to his self when Alice criticized his behavior. I am not saying that it is easy to hold on to yourself when someone you love is criticizing you, but it is possible.

First, you need to ask yourself if you are culpable. Be honest with yourself. See if there is some validity to the criticism. Fred was able to see that he was avoiding Alice because he felt criticized and would lose himself to her criticism.

If you are not culpable, then you have to ask yourself what is it that is really bothering you. The answer is typically emotional dependency. We react negatively to our partner's accusation because we want them to validate us. If we don't get their approval, we feel anxious and either submit to the person's pressure, pressure our partner to submit, withdraw, or stay connected and set our boundaries.

The other problem that I saw operating between Fred and Alice, and that I see in most troubled couples, is that Alice was mistaking Fred's desire as indicating his level of ability. In most areas of our lives we're readily able to differentiate between ability and desire. For example, we recognize that most fourteen-year-olds yearn to drive a car, but we don't assume their desire means they're capable of operating one. Yet in romantic relationships, we habitually confuse desire with ability. A person who says "I love you and care about you" may not know how to "care." Desires often outstrip abilities.

Sometimes we accuse a partner who loves us of not being interested. I've seen many relationships deteriorate when one partner accuses the other of being uninterested because they have a lack of love. Then the partners go off on an irrelevant tangent that's harmful to the very thing they think is missing, the true desire to love. Remember, the problem is more often a lack of ability than a lack of desire.

So what can you do if you recognize that you or the person in your life doesn't have the ability to fulfill your desires? First of all, be honest with what you want from him or her. Describe your disappointment within the context of what you do appreciate in your partner. This will lead to a discussion about the reality of who you are and what you can both do to change and make the relationship better. **The first person you should consult if you have a problem in the relationship is always your partner.** If you are still at an impasse, talk to friends who seem to be making their relationships work. The next step is seeking professional help.

SINCE I AM ONE HALF OF THE PERSON I WANT TO BE AND YOU ARE ONE HALF OF THE PERSON YOU WANT TO BE, TOGETHER WE WILL MAKE A WHOLE.

THE REALITY: A partner cannot make us whole. A partner can inspire us toward this goal but cannot do it for us.

This is a very romantic notion, but nonetheless unreasonable. Will joining half an orange and half a banana make a whole? The mathematics involved in relationships is different from the mathematics we learned in grade school. In school we learned that one-half plus one-half equals one, but in love it takes one plus one to make a solid relationship.

Of course this is the ideal. None of us is completely whole. We are all fragmented because we have disowned, projected or amputated parts of ourselves to survive, to please either our parents or our lovers, or to live up to some idealized image perpetuated to survive in our society.

When we fall in love with someone, we are seeing in that person the characteristics we need in ourselves. The paradigm explaining the romantic dynamic was originally constructed by Dr. Carl Jung and later elaborated on by psychologist Dr. Robert Johnson. In his book entitled *We: Understanding the Psychology of Romantic Love*, Dr. Johnson notes there is a feminine side (*anima*) and a masculine side (*animus*) in every individual.

Men are mostly masculine, so one of the basic attractions between a man and woman is that a man sees his dormant feminine side in her, and vice versa. This is the normal beginning of a relationship. But we need to remember that a relationship can only inspire us to develop ourselves. We still have to do the work ourselves.

When I expect you to complete me, I frustrate the forces within me. Gestalt therapists have demonstrated that we all have a built-in mechanism motivating us to become whole, to move toward completion and mastery. In a successful relationship, I will develop my shadow side (the underdeveloped side), and so will my partner.

For instance, if a woman is more sensitive than her partner and he is more assertive, she will become more assertive while he will become more sensitive.

I believe this dynamic underlies mate selection. We choose a partner who will create the types of challenges and pain that we need. If we digest these experiences in a therapeutic way, we will glean critical information that will facilitate and generate growth. Relationships fail when we don't understand the wisdom of our unconscious choices. When we lose sight of this perspective and inaccurately conclude that the struggle and pain have no value, the relationship enters a state of entropy and will eventually die.

CHAPTER 4

Destructive Communication: Some Straight Talk

o you want me to tell you something really subversive? Love is everything it's cracked up to be. That's why people are so cynical about it. . . . It really is worth fighting for, being brave for, risking everything for. And the trouble is, if you don't risk anything, you risk even more.

—ERICA JONG (1977)

In this chapter we will look at seven common communication patterns that sabotage relationships.

1. Needing to be right
2. Unfinished business

3. Tit-for-tat

4. Mind reading

5. The crimes of love

6. The emperor has no clothes

7. Psychological warfare

A word of caution: Don't be alarmed if you recognize one or more of these negative characteristics in your relationship with your partner. It doesn't mean that you have a "bad" relationship. However, it does suggest that you have some room for improvement. Remember, not one of us has a perfect relationship. A perfect relationship is a myth.

Professional golfer Tiger Woods doesn't practice his swing because it's poor. He practices to make a very good swing better. Like Tiger, we all have something to learn when it comes to improving our communication skills and enjoying healthier relationships. I like to say you don't have to be sick to get better.

Needing to Be Right

King of the Hill

As children, many of us played a heart-thumping, lung-popping game called King of the Hill. The king's goal was to maintain dominance over a particular territory. I don't know about your neighborhood, but in mine there were no rules of conduct. The king guarded his plot of land by shoving, kicking, punching or tripping any challenger.

This game, with its attendant ruthlessness, is not confined to children. And there are just as many queens battling for dominance as there are kings. Only the name of the game is different. When two adults play this game, it's called "I'm right and you're wrong." It begins with a difference of opinion and escalates. Both individuals in this sort of relationship are determined to be right all the time. I think of this as continual, mental street brawling. Neither party has any concept of negotiation, compromise or admission of error.

A couple stuck playing King of the Hill will argue about anything. The subject doesn't matter. What counts is winning. Each is willing to pay any cost to gain the upper hand. Often the quibbling and bickering evolves into verbal or physical abuse. The first phase of a quarrel usually begins with sophisticated intellectual and interpersonal maneuvers designed to outwit or one-up the partner. Typically men use logical argument to get their way, while women attempt to emotionally manipulate their partners into submission. I've heard many husbands hoping to put their wives in place by saying something like, "You're too emotional about this issue. Can't you see how illogical you are?" I've also seen many women force their husbands into submission by withholding sex, saying, "I just don't want to make love to you anymore."

If victory is not achieved with maneuvers at this level, then we usually resort to more destructive and primitive strategies to force surrender. These include:

➠ Psychological ploys like, "You are just like your mother!" or, "You treat me like I'm your father."

➠ Character assassinations like, "You never compromise. You are selfish."

➠ Verbal abuse like, "You are an idiot!" or "How can you be so stupid?"

➠ Physical abuse that includes slapping, punching, pinching, choking, spitting, pushing or physical restraint.

I remember treating a couple at a battered woman's shelter. Lydia and Saul were law students, so there was no doubt they were exceptionally bright. However, you wouldn't be able to tell how intelligent they were by observing their interaction. When relating to each other, their level of functioning was extremely low.

In one argument over breakfast Saul became frustrated because Lydia was uninterested in buying a time-share condominium. She argued that time-share condos limited vacation possibilities. Suddenly, Saul stood, opened the refrigerator and picked up a half-gallon of milk. He drank a mouthful, then turned and spat the milk in Lydia's face. Needless to say, Lydia stopped arguing. She began to cry. Saul had won, but at what price? Beneath all of his self-righteousness he was ashamed. He had humiliated a woman he loved and ravaged a relationship he treasured. Also, his own self-esteem and self-respect were crippled by his abusive behavior.

Individuals who need to be right are driven by insecurity and desperation. They spar as recklessly as a drowning person thrashes toward the shoreline. In their minds being wrong is equivalent to being an utter failure. Such people seem possessed.

They cast off all their values and personal integrity when they battle with their partners. It's easy to see how such an attitude destroys a relationship.

If you possess a consuming need to be right, you must learn that a relationship cannot survive if it is entirely dominated by your will. In order for a relationship to succeed, it must be large enough for two people, not one. I'll talk more about this in chapters 5 and 6.

Topdog and Underdog

A variation of King of the Hill is Topdog and Underdog. It works very simply. Topdog dominates, Underdog submits. Topdog makes every decision, wins every battle. Yet, while Underdog yields, secretly he or she resents what is happening and will express this discontent in some passive/indirect manner such as "forgetting" a birthday or neglecting to pick up Topdog's dry cleaning.

A couple may interchange roles at times, but one partner will be on top most of the time. Shifting roles does not alter the vertical structure of the relationship, which is the only kind of relationship either understands. Neither partner knows how to live in a horizontal "I to Thou" relationship, only how to take charge or to be submissive.

When a couple trapped in a vertical relationship comes to a therapist, invariably Topdog is surprised to learn there is a problem. He or she thinks everything is okay since the partner always "seems to agree with me." The key word is "seems." Underdogs agree with tyrants only to avoid the conflict inherent in challenges or to maintain Topdog's impression that he or she is always right. So we can see from this that Underdog is really the stronger partner, although this is not how it appears to the world. By withholding how he or she really feels from Topdog, Underdog is saying, "I don't think you can handle how I really feel. So I won't tell you. I'll just keep it my secret." You can see that Underdog is really in control of the relationship, even though he or she does not consciously realize it and want to admit it. Sometimes there is a payoff for being a victim.

The Cure for Needing to Be Right

It's extremely tragic, but many of us are caught in this trap. We want to be right—all the time. We don't want to be challenged; we don't want to admit that we are wrong.

The best cure I have found for this type of arrogance is taking the attitude to its absolute absurd extreme. Announce to your partner that you want to be right about EVERYTHING, that you KNOW EVERYTHING. Parodying your own behavior eases you and your partner. You are both able to recognize the absurdity of your imperial manner. Eventually you will both laugh at the preposterous notion that any human is eternally right. Humor is a miraculous method for extracting venom from personal relations.

We know that perfectionism underlies the need to be right. Therefore, another helpful intervention is to question the goal of perfectionism itself. Personally I have found this quite helpful. Is perfection truly what I want, or would it be more satisfying to strive to become MORE HUMAN? For me the answer always comes back a resounding "No" to the former and an emphatic "Yes" to the latter. When I labor to become more human, I'm able to crush my shameless pretensions of perfection.

My last suggestion concerns the perspective you have regarding what creates the problems in the relationship. In order to have a healthier relationship, it is necessary to look at all relationship problems as bilaterally generated. This means it is important to look at what you are doing rather than focus on your partner. Examine your role in the difficulty. What are you doing that contributes to this dynamic? What does this say about your emotional development and maturity? How are you supporting this problem? Are you avoiding facing the real issues in your relationship by avoiding confrontation?

Clearly, any relationship where one person has to be right is in trouble. That attitude makes it impossible to generate an atmosphere based on mutual respect. Respect is the minimum requirement of love. Without respect for individual differences, it is impossible to discover mutually satisfying solutions, which are the foundation of a healthy relationship.

Unfinished Business

Incomplete transactions occur when a couple begins talking about an issue but completes the discussion with the issue remaining unresolved. Such incomplete transactions damage relationships by creating unfinished business. In fact, incomplete transactions are the **hallmarks of a dysfunctional relationship**.

If your relationship suffers from this problem, you will notice that you are reluctant to engage your partner in a discussion because "it just doesn't do any good to talk about things." Or your resignation may be even deeper. You might discover that you don't even think about communicating with your partner anymore.

Other feelings typically evoked by incomplete transactions are frustration and anger. A person who reports, "We talk and talk and talk about things—but nothing ever seems to be settled. I hate getting into a discussion because it's useless. It's better to just not talk about our problems," is also frustrated and angry by the unfinished business.

There are several different communication patterns that contribute to this result. The first I will discuss is Changing Horses in Midstream.

Changing Horses in Midstream

The most common pattern of communication that ends in an incomplete transaction is changing horses in midstream. The dynamic is simple: *Instead of pursuing the topic under discussion, one partner changes topics and the other partner does not protest.* For example, if a woman approaches her husband about a problem she is having with the gardener, instead of responding to her comments, he may suddenly shift the conversation to overdue collections at work. She falls silent and accepts the dismissal. The result is an incomplete transaction.

Shifting subjects most often occurs when one person confronts the other about a behavior that he or she doesn't like. The person being confronted typically responds by saying something irrelevant. Imagine that you are confronting me about how I shift topics when you have something you want to share with me about your frustration with our relationship. If I respond by asking, "Do you think you will ever be happy with me?" I'd be attempting to shift the conversation to your insatiable character. I would shift the topic because I either wouldn't want to face the issue you are putting on the table or because I don't know how to deal with your criticism. Thus, the original topic is lost because I have changed the focus. An incomplete transaction takes place anytime the original topic is not addressed.

The next type of incomplete transaction pattern is called cross-complaining. As you will see, cross-complaining is a close cousin to changing horses in midstream.

Cross-Complaining

In this dynamic every time one person begins discussing an issue, the other person counters with a problem of his or her own. For example, I treated a couple who had not had intimate relations for over a year. Sherry had lost interest in having sex with Frank, and he was experiencing great pain over their distance. Every time Sherry attempted to raise an issue with Frank, like his staying out all night, Frank retaliated by referring to her lack of sexual desire. Because he was much better at verbal sparring than Sherry, her concerns were never taken seriously. Her frustration with him became one more reason to withhold sex. Unresolved and unexpressed resentment, frustration, and emotional dependency are sure means of decreasing sexual desire.

A couple entangled in a communication snarl develops what psychologist Martin Seligman terms "learned helplessness." Learned helplessness occurs when a person such as Sherry believes that an outcome is completely independent of her actions. In other words, if a person believes that no matter what she says or does the situation won't change—even though in reality the person does have the ability to influence an outcome—that person has acquired learned helplessness. If both partners suffer from this condition chronically, the relationship will deteriorate. Neither one will try to do anything to change what is wrong with the relationship. They will incorrectly conclude that nothing can be done about the problem. Remember, we see the world as we are, not as the world truly is.

The next dynamic also creates incomplete transactions, but not because there is a topic shift. It's because there was no connection whatsoever.

Two Ships Passing in the Night

There is an interesting phenomenon that occurs when two toddlers are playing together. It is called "parallel play." When two children are parallel playing, they are playing side-by-side but their play is unrelated. One child might be playing with farm animals while the other child is dialing calls on a toy telephone. At times their interactions may overlap, and the children will communicate with each other, but then each returns to his own play theme.

I've seen many adults mimic this behavior in their communication. They appear to be talking together, but in reality they are not. She's talking about one issue while he is talking about another. Here's an example.

Harry had been out of work for almost a year. During the first six months of unemployment, he tried to start a hobby shop, but it failed. For the past six months, he'd searched for a job. He and his wife, Katy, sold their house and recently borrowed money from Katy's parents to pay bills. A serious argument erupted when Katy tried to discuss a long-term plan with Harry. Her proposal was to generate additional capital by moving to a cheaper apartment and selling one car and some unnecessary furnishings. If they made these changes and liquidated some assets, they could exist on her salary for approximately one more year. If they didn't make these changes, the money they had borrowed would be gone in four months.

Harry reacted to Katy by laying out a short-term plan. His plan was based on the notion that within the next four months—"if we're lucky"—something should turn up. He then criticized her negativity and stated that it depressed him to think about liquidating some of their assets.

Obviously, this couple was talking about the same subject from very different perspectives. Harry was concerned with the next four months while Katy was focusing on a long-term solution. Harry completely missed Katy's point. Instead of reiterating her position, Katy just pouted and said, "You never listen to me." She felt disappointed and silently contemplated divorce.

It is impossible to find practical solutions if your discussions are parallel. The consequences of this problem are that both parties will usually feel frustrated and discouraged. Let's look at what can be done to deal with these bad habits.

The Cure for Incomplete Transactions

Curing incomplete transactions is simple in principle, but not easy in practice. The first step is becoming aware of the nature of your problem. Often partners have no idea of what's happening to their communication. All they know is that they just can't talk to each other. However, the actual problem usually is that they are **not taking care of one subject at a time**.

To find out if this is the case, appoint a discussion monitor. The monitor should be alert to digressions, ready to redirect the conversation to the agreed-upon topic in a cooperative, firm and inviting way. An example of typical phrasing is, "We have strayed off the subject; we need to settle the first issue. Let's decide if this new issue is more important than the first. If not, let's go back and finish the first issue before we discuss this one."

The logical choice for a monitor is the person who catches digressions from the topic more quickly. Sometimes both partners function as monitors. The selection method doesn't matter as long as the job is being done.

Some of you may be thinking, "What if it's not the kind of discussion you can resolve in two hours?" That's okay. You can agree on the fact that you can't resolve the issue right now and that you'd like to come back to it later. Sometimes it's better to take a break and gain some perspective before deciding what to do. Agreeing to take a break creates a temporary resolution to the problem. "We can't settle this right now. What we need to do is say that there is more to discuss. So let's figure out a time that's good for both of us, and then we can continue this discussion later."

Rescheduling a discussion is satisfactory as long as each person honors the agreement. Some transactions are incomplete because a participant doesn't keep the agreement. This person may say, "Okay, we'll talk about that later," but "later" never comes.

To reschedule a topic, you must be specific. You need to say, "How about 4:00 tomorrow? If you can't do it then, let's talk about the next time you can." Sometimes even this high degree of specificity doesn't work. At 4:00, one partner may be sitting in the den eager to talk while the other is upstairs watering plants. The one downstairs may become angry. **Don't just sit there and wait for your partner to give you what you want.** Instead go upstairs and say, "It's 4:00. It's time for us to finish discussing the issue we started to talk about yesterday." (It's also okay to say you don't like the fact that he or she isn't taking responsibility for the agreement, but don't get sidetracked unless that subject is truly more important for you than the original one.)

Be aware of priorities as you monitor your conversations. Some topics are more important than others. For example, imagine you are deciding who's going to take on a particular job for remodeling the house. The subject is the division of labor in terms of the project. However, in the course of that discussion, you begin to wonder whether you want to stay in the relationship. You wonder if it might not be better to sell the house and terminate the relationship.

Now the most relevant topic becomes your feelings about ending the relationship. When an important new issue arises, you and your partner need to be flexible enough to respond to it. However, before you change subjects, there must be consensus. You can say something to your partner like, "Maybe we need to redirect our discussion. For me, [the new topic] is more pertinent to our discussion right now. Would you agree?" There should be agreement when changing the subject. Unilateral shifts create a different kind of trouble, which I will cover later in this chapter.

Transferring attention from the remodeling job to continuation of the relationship makes sense. **There are subjects that, when resolved, will settle the other issues.** What we're searching for in our dialogue with each other is the subject that has the greatest degree of relevance in our lives, the one that encompasses all the other situations that distress us.

For example, stating "I don't like the way you talk to me" is insufficient. A more significant way to approach this subject is to make a more personal statement: "I feel so worthless because I don't set boundaries regarding what I will and won't tolerate in the way that you talk to me. I don't like being a victim! I would like to have a conversation in which I don't feel threatened, where we are speaking to each other on equal terms and with respect. I will let you know if you are crossing this line with me, and hopefully you will respect my boundaries." Obviously, the latter statement is more specific and more likely to create a solution.

Such interaction takes a lot of practice. We didn't learn it from our families because our parents usually avoided talking about personal issues in our presence. They were told by their parents that children should be protected from conflict. They were wrong! **Children don't need to be protected from conflict. They need adults to show them how to meet conflict head-on and resolve it.**

Conflict met in the right way often facilitates a solution rather than continued confrontation. An incident that came up during a recent therapy session demonstrates how a couple discovered deeper themes in their lives. Alex is a musician/artist, and Gail is an executive secretary. They have two children. They have been together ten years, although at the time of this session they had been separated for about six months.

The session started with Alex exploring what he called a "death wish." As he clarified his thoughts, what emerged was not a fear of death but a fear that as soon as everything in his life was good, some disaster would take everything away. Alex's sense of foreboding made him afraid of success and made him afraid of wanting. He believed that as soon as he achieved a goal, its reward would vanish. As we talked, Alex discovered that his fear created foreboding that became a self-fulfilling prophecy. This was his way of protecting himself from disappointment. Unconsciously, Alex ensured that he would not be successful because then he would start to want to want.

I asked what early experiences could have contributed to his self-destructive patterns.

"Maybe I feel this way because we moved so much?" Alex recalled moving twelve times in the first ten years of his life. Each time he made friends in a new neighborhood, the family moved once again. It was easy to see how these childhood experiences contributed to his desire to be wantless and needless. He had been carrying unexpressed grief and pain all his adult life.

His marriage to Gail did not improve the situation because Gail protected him from facing unpleasant feelings. Whenever Alex started to approach his pain, she became flippant. "Oh, you know, I just kind of say, 'There goes Alex again, talking about his fear of death,' and we just laugh about it."

"I think that's very sad," I told her.

"Well, we just laugh about it, and I know I may sound cold and flippant, but, you know. . . ."

"You *are* cold and flippant," I said. "I think that this reflects what's missing between you two in terms of your relationship. You don't want to see the terrible pain that's in your husband."

As I spoke, Alex started to cry. Then Gail began to cry, too. I asked Gail why she was crying. She replied, "Because he seems to be in pain."

"I don't think that's the only thing you're crying about," I told her. "I think this subject touches something deep inside of you, too. You're not just feeling his pain."

When I said this, she sobbed harder. Although she still didn't know what the pain was, she, too, had moved to a deeper level. **It is when we get to these deeper levels that we can heal and discover solutions.** Sometimes the solutions do not involve taking action. Often they come from discovering and sharing with our partners our personal unmet desires. An incredible liberation accompanies such self-disclosure.

Many times the solution comes from listening, from being completely present with your partner and experiencing empathy for him or her. That's hard for people to understand. We are action-oriented. We want to know what we can do to help. Frequently, when people say they want to talk, they mean they need to get to a deeper understanding and acceptance. For example, Alex would have liked to hear Gail say, "Gee, honey, it must be terrible to live with that fear." But regardless of whether he received empathy from Gail, Alex needed to learn how to support himself, how to soothe his own pain and anxiety about losing those people or things that were important to him. In this way he could be more empathic and compassionate for himself.

Many people enter therapy with the goal of getting in touch with their feelings. In my opinion that is not an appropriate goal. Your job in therapy is to find out what you need to say. When you find the words that are true for your life, you'll get in touch with your feelings. **When we touch a truth about our lives, there is a strong, uncontrollable emotional reaction.**

In a healthy relationship, both partners strive to help each other find the personal statements that will heal. If your partner does not encourage you, or doesn't want to participate in this search for your personal voice, do it anyway. Remember, it's your emotional dependency that demands that your partner needs to do it with you. Focusing on what you need to do will always be in the best interest of your relationship.

Tit-for-Tat

Any relationship between two people becomes deadlocked when they engage in tit-for-tat bargaining. In this type of conflict, both argue that they would change if only the other would make some change first. A man may say, "If only my wife were more careful with money, I would be more generous." Or a woman may say, "If only my husband were more considerate, I would be less demanding." In tit-for-tat language, the key words are "if only" and "I would." Between these bookends any message can be inserted.

What happens in the tit-for-tat configuration is that every action one person takes is dependent on what the other person is or is not doing, and vice versa. Often, what you'll hear from a couple struggling with this issue is, "Well, I'm not going to change unless he changes first." It's like arguing about which came first, the chicken or the egg. The couple quibbles endlessly over who caused the problem or who needs to change first. If one gets angry with the other or acts in some untoward manner, he or she will justify the behavior by saying something like, "Well, I'm angry because you're angry," or "I did this because you did that." In this sort of relationship, neither party is taking responsibility for their behavior. Each justifies his or her own actions by citing what the other person is or isn't doing. This deadly communication system obstructs any change in the partnership.

Before attempting to improve such a relationship, you must first consider what would happen if the desired changes were actually made. Imagine that one mate says to another, "You know, you just don't take care of yourself. You've gotten fat. You are not attractive to me anymore. I don't want to make love to you anymore." The person making the complaint should think through with his or her partner the effect of the desired changes. The overweight partner might say, "Let's say I become nice and thin and sexy. What's that going to do? What's going to happen in this relationship? How does that change us? What will that create in our relationship?"

Jessica wanted her husband, Eric, to be thinner and more attractive. She wanted him to work out, lose twenty pounds, tighten up and wear more stylish clothes. The question is, if Eric changes along these lines, how will she be affected? Eric may become very appealing to younger women. Is Jessica ready to deal with competition? Will she become jealous? Is Eric still going to want the relationship after he starts receiving attention from other women? *A change in one person will inevitably upset the status quo of a relationship.*

Often when we complain, we don't think about what will

happen when things start to change. If we actually considered the implications of change, most of us would discover that the issues we are complaining about serve some kind of function in our lives. Eric's extra weight meant that he was less likely to be attractive to other women, so Jessica felt more secure. I am certain she wasn't conscious of this, but it was a factor in their relationship.

Sometimes a change in a partner might not benefit us. When we honestly explore the nature of our complaints, we can take responsibility for our share of the problems and stop heaping blame on our partners.

In the case of alcoholism, for instance, it's easy for a co-dependent person to reason, "My problem is my partner's drinking, and if my partner just stopped drinking, all our problems would be resolved." But what we find in recovering families is that sobriety isn't always the cure-all for relationship problems. The drinking is just the scapegoat for other problems that plague the marriage. You can imagine the shock when a family discovers that drinking isn't the only problem. The alcoholic is usually angry; he or she has given up drinking, but the conflicts are still there. And the co-alcoholic says something like, "I did say your drinking was the problem, but now I still don't like you. And I can't blame it on the drinking anymore."

The drinking problem must be treated before the partners can identify what other problems exist independent of the drinking. Alcohol distorts everything the way a fun house mirror does. Until the images are flattened out, dealing with these other issues is impossible.

It is true that many of the actions of a codependent spouse are triggered by their partner's drinking. We are all influenced by our partner's behavior, whether negatively or positively; all behavior in a relationship is determined bilaterally. But to say that **all behavior is contingent on another person's actions is false and leads to an impasse in the relationship**.

The Cure for the Tit-for-Tat Syndrome

The only way to break out of a system built on blame is for each person to take responsibility for his or her own action. **The only person you can directly change is *yourself*.** You will never change if you're waiting for your partner to change, and vice versa.

Verbal abuse provides a good example of how the blaming cycle operates. Here's how one of my patients dealt with an abusive husband who humiliated her in front of friends by saying she was stupid. Jane and I spent a therapy session role-playing an appropriate response. The next time Jane and her husband went out to dinner with friends, as soon as there was an incident of verbal abuse, Jane said, "I don't like it when you say I'm stupid in front of our friends. I'm sure it makes them feel as uncomfortable as it makes me feel. If you do this again, I'm leaving and taking a cab home. We can talk when you come home."

Later in the evening, her husband again said something derogatory. Jane folded her dinner napkin and said, "I told you before, I will not tolerate this type of behavior. It makes me uncomfortable, and I'm sure it makes our friends uncomfortable too. I refuse to be treated this way. I'm leaving, and we'll talk when you get home." Then she left. She may have to leave a few more restaurants before her husband gets the message and changes his behavior.

But this much is certain: The problem would continue if Jane only complained about his behavior, even though she'd be justified. She must keep communicating her displeasure actively and set appropriate boundaries.

The message I would like to leave you with in terms of breaking free of the tit-for-tat syndrome is to let the best of you do the thinking and talking. If you can stay centered and focus on who you want to be as a partner, regardless of how your partner is behaving, then you will break this negative cycle.

Mind Reading

A mind reader claims he or she knows you better than you know yourself. This person is convinced he or she understands all your feelings and motivations. Even when you try to give this person information that suggests otherwise, he or she just discounts it.

I recall a session with a husband and wife named Gerald and Sandra. Gerald explained to me that Sandra didn't feel comfortable if he went to bed before she did. He said Sandra would purposely come into the bedroom and wake him so he would be present with her. He theorized that Sandra was not comfortable enough to fall asleep unless someone else was awake in the house. He was positive that Sandra was insecure.

I asked Sandra to respond to Gerald's comments. She turned to him and said, "There are some times when I just miss you and I want to interact with you." She started to explain these late-evening awakenings as her desire to connect with him. And then an interesting thing came out. Gerald had a moment of clarity. "Maybe it's because I'm half asleep and it will be easier to talk to me."

But then he reverted to his earlier position. "No. I know you do it all the time just because somebody's got to be awake. You wake me up and start to talk to me, and then go to sleep." Because Sandra went to sleep after waking him up, he concluded that she didn't want to talk with him. But more was to be revealed that day in my office.

As it turned out, the reason Sandra stopped talking to Gerald was because he'd get upset. She would say something like, "I wonder why you don't kiss me before we have sex anymore," and Gerald would spring from bed angrily and say, "Okay, we'd better talk about this."

Then Sandra's desire to talk would collapse. "I'll go to sleep," she'd say. "I'll just go to sleep."

What I see happening between Sandra and Gerald is her desire to discuss something that is bothering her, but she starts her conversation with a criticism. She's hoping to address something that is bothering her, but when Gerald reacts like a grizzly bear, Sandra wants to hibernate. She avoids him by going to sleep. He interprets this as, "Well, she just wants me awake so she can go to sleep." And no matter what she told him in our session about how she really felt, he knew better. That's amazing, isn't it? He believed he knew better than Sandra what she was feeling. This is typical mind-reader behavior.

Here's the scenario of another couple whose relationship was being destroyed by mind reading. Judy and Philip came to therapy because of sexual difficulties. Philip's sexual appetite had decreased, and when they did have sex, he couldn't maintain an erection.

When I asked them what they thought was going on, Philip said Judy didn't enjoy sex. He said she just wanted to get into the thrusting part of the sexual experience. Then he turned to Judy and said, "You're not orgasmic. You just want to hurry and get it over."

When Judy asked how he could possibly know whether she'd had an orgasm, he responded, "You don't flush. The other women I've been with flushed when they had an orgasm." He was telling her about her subjective sexual experience!

The truth was that Judy enjoyed intercourse more than fore-play. She explained that she preferred what she called "after play" and that she was not frigid. However, Philip remained convinced that Judy was frigid in spite of what she told him. He didn't want to know how sexual Judy really was. It scared him. He wasn't sure that he would be able to satisfy her.

When a partner says, "I think I know what's going on with you," it doesn't matter what you have to say. How will the two of you ever deal with anything? The relationship becomes a soliloquy. A mind-reading act kills the possibility for intimate connection.

The Cure for the Mind-Reading Act

The best cure for this dynamic is to immediately deal with every mind-reading act by confronting your partner with comments such as, "You're talking for me, and I feel disconnected from you. I don't like to be disconnected from you. I want to tell you what I want and what I like. If you imagine you know what I want, please check out your hunches with me." **You must do**

this every time your partner attempts to read your mind, regardless of whether he or she is right. Remember to change your approach if it does not work, and you need to change your approach as many times as it takes to get the results you want.

For example, if your partner anticipates one of your needs, you can say something like, "I appreciate you being concerned about my needs, but I'd be able to appreciate your thoughtfulness even more if you would take the time and ask me what I'd like."

The principle that should guide you in this type of a confrontation is to **compliment the positive intention in your partner's behavior, then discourage the mind reading, and finally ask for what you want.** This kind of a confrontation honors your partner's dignity and informs your partner about your personal preferences, making it much easier for him or her to respond to your desires.

The Crimes of Love

My mentor, Dr. Kempler, originally discussed the concept he called "Crimes of Love." These are destructive acts that are committed with quite good intentions. As children we all learn to categorize experiences and objects. For example, we learn to categorize animate and inanimate objects. Another classification we are taught at an early age is good and bad. We label behaviors and emotions as good and bad according to the implicit rules of our families and our culture.

With very little variation, we could agree on what behaviors and feelings should be classified as good or bad. On the one side of the coin are good traits and emotions: love, generosity, kindness, joy, happiness, helpfulness and honesty. On the other side of the coin are cruelty, selfishness, hatred, mistrust, resentment, stinginess and pain. The fact that we can get a consensus on this list demonstrates that we are taught these categories with some kind of social agreement.

However, when I ask an audience to consider an actual situation with an alcoholic female and a male adult child of an alcoholic family, the distinctions between good and bad eventually begin to blur. Let's take a look at how this happens.

This couple began their marriage as people usually do; they tried to be good people in their marriage. Yet Suzie was an alcoholic and brought into the marriage a propensity toward the use of alcohol, especially when a crisis would occur in her life. After three years of marriage, her mother died suddenly and Suzie was thrown into an individual crisis. The relationship with her mother was poor, and she was filled with guilt and pain. When she turned to her husband to process her feelings, he wasn't able to be much help. He avoided dealing with his own feelings and didn't know how to support his wife. She eventually turned to what always worked; she turned to alcohol, which started to cause many problems in several areas of her life.

Her ability to fulfill her role in the family diminished. Because she desired to be of value to her family, she felt horrible that she was not functioning well and therefore she drank more. She was caught in a vicious cycle, and it is predictable that her well-intentioned husband, who was an adult child of an alcoholic, compensated for her impairment. He assumed the responsibilities that she was neglecting.

His childhood experiences with an alcoholic mother served as a model for dealing with his wife. The unspoken contract was, "When you step down, I'll go ahead and step up. If you're not taking care of the kids, I'll do that. If you don't straighten up the house, don't worry, I'll clean it up. If you are unable to go to work, I'll call in sick for you."

He became his wife's social worker. As these dynamics escalated, he moved toward sainthood. When he reached it, she became the unredeemed sinner. At this point in the cycle, she began feeling even worse because of how "good" her husband was and how "rotten" or "bad" she was.

However, she wasn't able to say anything to him about her resentment because she felt she didn't have the right to be angry or upset. Gratitude and shame were choking her to death.

This cycle is the crime of love. The husband was not acting out of bad intentions. Suzie's behavior didn't begin because she made a decision to ruin her husband's life. Nobody does that. And her husband wasn't acting like a saint in order to make her feel miserable. They were both trying to be "good people," but before they realized what hit them, they found themselves caught up in a devastating pattern. Because they were enmeshed in their concern about what was good and bad, they no longer were of value to each other.

The Cure for the Crimes of Love

The entire problem of this pattern is based on trying to be good. In reality, there are no good or bad feelings. Feelings simply exist. Sometimes they're effective and helpful in a situation, sometimes they get in the way and sometimes they are unnecessary. In the situation of the alcoholic and codependent, we can see that love, generosity and kindness are more harmful than helpful. In this situation, it would have been better for the husband to have been more self-concerned, a bit less kind and more distrustful. At some point, he should have said, "We have a problem, and it needs to be addressed. I'm not living like this anymore. Let's get some help." Instead of over-functioning and compensating for his wife's problem, he needed to define his boundaries. Defining your boundaries is therapeutic for both you and your relationship.

Keep in mind that relationships are bilateral: When there is a problem in a relationship, it's because both partners are creating and supporting the issue. If one partner no longer plays the prescribed role in the situation, the equilibrium is disrupted. A crisis erupts in the relationship, and an opportunity for change follows.

The Emperor Has No Clothes

This problem occurs when a couple has a tacit agreement to totally support and agree with each other no matter what. It's similar to the emperor who ordered a tailor to make him the finest royal robe in the world. The tailor resented the emperor's abuse of his power and made nothing. To embarrass the emperor, he presented a box that apparently contained his creation. He pretended to remove the most regal coat in all the land and place this invisible coat on the emperor's shoulders, telling him how wonderful he looked. The emperor accepted the coat because he thought he was the only one who couldn't see it. In fact he looked incredibly silly standing around in his under-wear. Yet all of his servants and nobles were afraid to tell him the truth, that there was no robe.

In a relationship, the emperor's new clothes are the semblance of complete agreement and mutuality in the partnership. Neither partner ever challenges the other. They never disagree. They never question the other. Everything in the partnership is hunky-dory. Most couples who live by this principle are extremely proud they get along so well. But it's a ruse.

The truth is that their mutuality is a facade as transparent as the emperor's robe. On close examination, you will find one individual who is afraid to state how he or she really feels, terri-fied of exposing a rift in the harmony of the relationship. This individual is horrified by conflict and therefore complies with everything the partner desires.

The Cure for the Emperor's New Clothes

There is no easy cure for this problem. First you need to get honest with yourself that you are living a lie. Is this truly the way you want to spend the rest of your life? If you hit rock bottom with this behavior, you may become willing to take a risk and tell the truth. No two people are always going to agree. Therefore, to begin changing this pattern of communication it is important to share your fear of what might happen if you don't agree with your partner. Be prepared, however, because your partner will likely exert pressure on you to keep the status quo. Remember, emotional fusion requires that the person close to you thinks and feels exactly the same way you do. If your partner does react in this manner, try to express an understanding of his or her fear, saying something like, "I'm sure you are concerned that our relationship may end if we don't agree with each other all the time. I'm afraid too, and I don't want to live like this any longer. I'll do whatever I can do to help make this a positive improvement for our relationship, but I can't do your work for you." Your acknowledgment, reassurance and commitment to the relationship may provide enough inspiration for your partner to find a way to soothe his or her own anxiety and become more open to finding a better way to live.

I want to make a note here regarding power in relationships. Appearances are very deceiving when it comes to who wields the most power. It is usually true that the person who appears to have all the power in a relationship doesn't. In the situation described above, it is the person who is withholding his or her disagreement who has the power. From the outside, it appears as if the person who always speaks his or her mind exerts control, but he or she doesn't. You see, the partner who is withholding is really the more powerful person. He or she perceives the partner as being incapable of coping with differences. The fear that stops them from sharing what they truly feel or think is the belief that the other person will not be able to cope with their differences.

Psychological Warfare

Dr. Gerald Zuk, one of the founders of the family therapy movement, observed a phenomenon among family members he called "silence-inducing strategies." These interpersonal maneuvers are designed to reduce conflict and end transactions by silencing your partner.

The most obvious silence-inducing strategy is achieved through labeling a person or dismissing his or her feelings. Telling someone that he or she shouldn't feel a certain way is a prime example. An even more abusive silence-inducing strategy is name-calling. Calling someone stupid or selfish or an idiot is an interpersonal maneuver designed to shut the other person up.

Sometimes couples even utilize therapy to silence their partners. I see this happen between couples in therapy. Probably the most common ploy is, "I'm going to bring this up with Dr. Berger." This threat usually stops the spouse dead in his or her tracks, contemplating the hot seat they are going to sit in at the next therapy session. A partner who makes such a comment is using therapy as a threat. And what's incredible is that this person is surprised when his or her partner does not want to continue treatment. Who would want to remain in therapy when it is constantly being used against them?

I want to say that I have seen this strategy used in a positive way, too. To stop an escalation some couples say, "Let's table this discussion until we meet with Dr. Berger. We don't seem to be getting anywhere, and it seems that things are just heating up between us." Once again, the motive for your behavior is critical.

How to Stop Psychological Warfare

There are two ways to stop someone from silencing you. The first is to immediately object to the maneuver by saying, "I don't like you labeling me selfish when I am trying to express something I want in our relationship. Whether I am selfish or not, I have a right to let you know what I want!" This kind of assertiveness is extremely helpful in dealing with a partner who attempts to silence you with labels. If the labeling crosses over and becomes verbally abusive, it is important to assertively set a boundary to stop this violation. "I don't like you calling me a bitch, and I won't tolerate it. If you don't like what I am saying to you, tell me that. But I won't sit still while you put me down and verbally abuse me. I hope that, after you calm down, you will be able to show me more respect."

The second technique is to move the discussion to a level above the content of your interaction. In psychological parlance, this is referred to as meta-communication. **This means that you are looking at how you are communicating rather than what you are communicating.** This technique works best when you and your partner have already established an understanding about this destructive process and have made a commitment to find more effective ways to communicate. Then this technique can be very effective if it is applied at the first sign of a silence-inducing strategy.

Charlie and Sue entered therapy at Sue's insistence. She was tired of being verbally abused and shut down by Charlie's attacks. Sue had come from a rather wealthy family and was used to a very high standard of living. Charlie was a self-made man. Through his hard work he had done exceptionally well in his career and he now was earning a six-figure salary, but he was extremely stingy. When Sue noticed some unusual symptoms in their three-year-old son, she told Charlie she wished to take the boy to a particular pediatrician. Charlie was furious. "You're spoiled, Sue," he said. "You can't just go and take our child to the most expensive specialists. I'm not rich like your family." He insisted that Sue take Ron to an internist whose fee was considerably less than that of the doctor she wished to consult.

Sue submitted to Charlie's request because she didn't want to be "spoiled," and the results were nearly tragic. As it turned out, the internist misdiagnosed the child's heart condition, and he nearly died in the emergency room before having open-heart surgery to repair a valve. Sue was unable to forgive herself for endangering her child because she did not stand up to Charlie.

Needless to say, the first session with this couple was extraordinarily intense. Charlie was a very strong-willed individual who felt justified in the way he interacted with his wife. I challenged Charlie regarding the way he "indirectly manipulated her to get what he wanted." After an hour of intense interaction, he began to see the insidious manner he was utilizing to control Sue and get what he wanted.

The next phase of therapy included helping Sue and Charlie learn how to talk about how they were communicating as a way of correcting this dysfunctional habit. Sue became very good at bringing this dynamic to Charlie's attention as an ally, without polarizing. She would interrupt him whenever he began to put her down and remind him that he didn't have to put her down to ask for what he wanted. She would reassure him that she was interested in pleasing him and would take his ideas and desires into serious consideration. Sue's intervention was highly effective and has decreased the psychological warfare considerably.

Learn from Sue. When you request that your partner stop and look at how he or she is communicating, it is most effective if you intervene as an ally. If you polarize your partner, this will be an exercise in futility.

CHAPTER 5

Guidelines for Healthy Communication

mmature love says: "I love you because I need you." Mature love says: "I need you because I love you."

— ERICH FROMM (1956)

ou can hold yourself back from the sufferings of the world, that is something you are free to do and it accords with your nature, but perhaps this very holding back is the one suffering you could avoid.

— FRANZ KAFKA (1917)

Poor communication habits plague almost everyone. Yet even when we admit to our own failings, most of us persist in believing that our partners have certain abilities they do not in fact possess. This creates a mystique infected with misleading expectations.

No one is very good at talking about personal matters. In my personal and clinical experiences, even an eloquent person capable of dazzling dinner guests with an analysis of foreign policy during the main course or beguiling them with a wistful anecdote about a three-legged dog stranded on a traffic island during dessert falls silent when the subject becomes intimate.

The effects of healthy and unhealthy communication have been studied extensively. Researchers have found that direct and positive communication patterns are prevalent in healthier, more successful families and relationships, whereas indirect and negative communication patterns occur in troubled families or relationships. Communication is the foundation upon which a relationship unfolds.

One of the observations I have made as I have worked with families and couples over the last two decades is that all of us would like to have good relationships. Anyone will tell you, "Sure, I'd like a healthy relationship!" It's a goal we'd all like to achieve, but we lack the daring and necessary skills to make it happen, and so we fall painfully short.

Our parents passed on the best of what they knew, but they could only transmit what they learned, often from inadequate models. This doesn't mean they are or were bad people. Quite the contrary. They, like us, did the best they could with what they knew.

Some of you who grew up in families where emotional dependency was rampant and communication was poor may feel hopeless about changing. You may be thinking to yourself, *I'll never be able to learn how to communicate in a better way.* If you continue to hide behind this despair, you won't learn how to communicate better. But if you are willing to grow up, take risks, and commit yourself to saying what you want or need to say, then you will be well on your way.

The real obstacle to better communication is emotional dependency. Your dependency determines what you will and won't say. It also determines what you do and don't invite your partner to talk about with you.

Emotional dependency demands that all communication be based on reciprocity. This dependency-based expectation states, "I'll be open and vulnerable, but you must, too." Your partner must respond in a certain manner for you to feel safe. This demand will never create the security you want. Your security needs to be determined by what you do, not what your partner does.

We are all capable of growing up. But not all of us will, because it means taking risks. If you want to walk on the wild side, I have some guidelines for you. Warning: The following guidelines are not for the faint of heart.

Make Statements
Rather Than Ask Questions

Stop asking questions! Asking a question is often an indirect way of telling someone how you feel. Many of us don't realize that we are hiding behind our questions because this bad habit becomes automatic after several years of practice. We ask questions rather than speak what's on our minds.

Here's a typical situation. The two of you are drinking coffee and reading the Sunday newspaper. You are quite content until your partner begins whistling tunelessly as he flips through the metro section. You find you are absolutely unable to concentrate with this annoying disruption so you ask, "Why are you whistling?"

This is classic ineffective and indirect communication. You do not care why your spouse is whistling! You want him or her to stop, and you are not being straight about it. You are not expressing what you really want. It would be far more effective to say, "Honey, I am having difficulty concentrating on what I'm reading. I want to know if you'd be willing to stop whistling. If you aren't willing to stop, I'll find a quieter spot in the house."

As with all forms of ineffective behavior, we have learned these bad habits legitimately. Whatever the cause of the problem, the solution is simple. Since we have difficulty stating what we want in a clear, concise and straightforward manner, we have to practice. For example, if in response to your partner embarrassing you at a party, you say, "Why did you mention my difficulty with my weight?" you are not letting your partner know how you really feel. It would be more effective and more direct to say, "I don't want you to discuss in public my concerns with my weight!"

One therapeutic directive I often give couples who are habitually asking questions rather than making declarations is, "Questions are off limits for the next week." I tell the pair they must communicate only by making declarations and statements for the next seven days.

Here's how this type of intervention works. Raul was a computer repairman in his early thirties who was quite successful at work, but at home he became soft and unassertive. He told me resented his wife, Alberta, for "controlling his life," but he was ambivalent about standing up for himself. He feared Alberta would leave him if he became "aggressive." The anxiety Raul experienced can be understood as energy he was blocking from expression. When we become excited, regardless of the nature of the excitement, and we stop ourselves from expressing this excitement, it will turn into anxiety.

Raul had been attempting to stand up for himself by asking questions. He'd say things like, "Why are you always telling me what to do?" or "Why don't you let me make my own decisions?"

During one session he described how angry he'd been with his father during his childhood. He hated the way his father allowed his mother to control their lives. You can see that there were many therapeutic paths I could have pursued in working with Raul's unassertive behavior. I could have had him talk to his father about his anger, explore the abandonment issue or acknowledge his dependency. However, I have found taking action in an immediate situation is more effective than returning to the past. Therefore, I pointed out the similarity between Raul's behavior and his father's, and then instructed him to make some outrageous declarations to Alberta. His first few attempts were timid, but he quickly got the hang of it and started telling her what he wanted from the marriage. He went from, "Boy, this is really hard to do. I'm not used to telling you what I want" to "I'm sick and tired of you telling me what to do! I don't like how controlling you are! I don't need your help all the time. When I do, I will ask you for it!"

The dilemma Raul confronted in his marriage is one familiar to many men today: A man cannot ask his wife to let him grow up. A man has to make his own declaration of independence.

When our country was being conceived, we didn't ask England to give us our independence. We demanded it! We made a Declaration of Independence.

If you find yourself compulsively asking questions of your partner, try following the directive described above for one week. *Make a conscious decision to refrain from asking questions and to replace your questions with positive statements that reflect your personal desires and declare what you want.* Changing your behavior will be difficult initially, but with some consistent practice, especially with your partner, you can form a new habit quickly.

I also want to warn you that when you shift how you function in your relationship, your relationship will change too. Even though this is a change for the better, it may at first be experienced negatively by your partner. If this is the case, your partner is likely to try to make you return to the usual way of doing business. He or she is not a bad person for attempting to sabotage your growth, just responding to the forces of equilibrium that are at work in all relationships. Remember, the reason you are behaving differently is that you want to be a better person, rather than to get a merit badge from your partner. So hold on to yourself even though he or she may attempt to sabotage your efforts.

Deliver Your Message to the Proper Person

Often we relate our feelings or frustrations to the wrong person. We complain to our friends about our partners, or we talk to our partners about our friends, or we go into individual therapy and discuss both our partners and our friends with a therapist. All of these communications are forms of gossip, and gossip is destructive because it deflects us from direct expression.

A very simple yet important communication rule is to deliver your message to the proper person. Most of the time the proper subject for our message will be clear. If you are upset with your wife's laziness, then you need to speak with her directly rather than talk to a friend. If you are disturbed by a neighbor's habitual lateness when she drives the car pool, you need to discuss your annoyance with her directly.

At times the true target of our message may be less obvious. Sometimes we may be saying something to our partner that is really meant for ourselves. For instance, if I am angry about letting my wife undermine my authority with my children by contradicting me before the children, then the issue I really have is with myself and not with her. I need to talk with myself about how I can better take care of myself and not blame my wife for what she has done to me.

Gossip is ubiquitous in our society because it creates the illusion that something is being done about a problem. People feel better when they have dumped their frustration, but the improvement is only temporary. It's a Band-Aid, and it doesn't resolve the dynamic that has caused the problem in the first place.

Sadly, in some forms of individual therapy, gossip has been institutionalized. However, since I believe, as do most family-oriented therapists, that we cope much more effectively with life when we learn how to communicate in a direct and positive manner, I typically discourage individual therapy with someone who's in a serious, committed relationship. I made this professional decision for two reasons. The first is that I'd be sending the message to my patient that it's not better to deal directly with their partner. I would be passing up an important opportunity to help my patient learn how to communicate more effectively with someone he or she loves. Second, if I treated someone in individual therapy who is in a serious relationship, I'd be harming that relationship. By allowing my client to talk with me instead of his or her partner, I'd be siphoning off intimacy from their relationship. There'd be an implicit message to the partner that he or she is not of value. This message undermines the natural therapeutic value and importance of the relationship.

The reality is that individual therapy is a myth. As the individual changes in the course of individual therapy, his or her intimate relationships will also change. Remember that the dynamics in relationships are determined bilaterally. Therefore, if one person behaves differently, his or her partner's behavior must change too.

Deliver the Whole Message

Most communications are incomplete. We communicate only a part of what we really want to say, usually just the tip of the iceberg. We almost always omit the most relevant information. Sometimes we lack an awareness of what we really want or desire. In this case, developing and honing self-awareness will help you communicate more directly. At other times, we may be conscious of what we want to say but are afraid to say it, fearing our partner's displeasure or hurt feelings. Here again the face of emotional dependency rears its ugly head. Regardless of our motivation, we need to realize that it is both dishonest and disrespectful to conceal important information from our partners.

This is a controversial issue, even among professionals, especially when someone has had an affair. A question I often hear is, "Should I tell my spouse I had an affair?" Professional opinions on this matter vary. They range from "definitely not" to "it is imperative to be honest." I'm more aligned with the latter position when there's a desire to reconcile. Here's why.

Providing your partner with the truth is important for several reasons. First, you cannot have true trust in a relationship unless you are completely honest with your partner. Trust is based on the knowledge that the two of you will mutually discuss all relevant and important issues and information regarding the relationship.

Second, by concealing your affair you are disrespecting your partner. Not informing your partner is tantamount to telling him or her, "I don't think you can handle the truth." In my clinical experience, I've discovered that people cope with the truth much better than deceptions or illusions.

Third, you are not giving your partner the necessary information to address what is really happening in the relationship and to make an informed decision. Without being told about the affair, your partner will never know how serious your difficulties really are, and therefore the two of you will never be able to make a serious effort to work out these problems. An affair is the smoke; it is not the fire. You cannot put out the fire unless you admit and recognize that the fire is burning.

People don't just go out and have an affair. The affair is a symptom that something is missing from the relationship. If your partner does not know what has been happening in the relationship, then how can he or she decide whether to stay or leave? When a person is told the truth, then he or she has a choice regarding whether to salvage the relationship. Having this choice is very important. It allows the "victim of the betrayal" to regain control over his or her life.

Anytime you withhold the truth about an affair, or any other matter, you also compromise your own integrity. An act of omission is as much a lie as an act of commission.

Omissions prevent mutually satisfying resolutions to problems. For instance, when our partners do not follow through on a promise, we usually get angry and stop there, but we shouldn't. The rest of the message is also important. We need to go through the anger to the other side into the underlying feelings. We need to express all of the elements of our disappointment in order to get to the truth. Anger is a secondary emotion. Behind anger always lies disappointment, pain or fear. When I work with a patient who is extremely angry, I help the person explore the underlying feelings. Delivering the whole message is the only way that a person can resolve chronic anger.

Listen with Both Your Eyes and Your Ears

Listening is an integral part of communicating. If you do not listen well, it is impossible for you to respond relevantly to your partner. But listening involves more than just hearing what the other person is saying. It also requires listening to what is not being stated and listening with your eyes. It probably sounds strange that I ask you to listen with your eyes, but let me explain.

It is important to look at your partner as he or she speaks to you because, in addition to his or her verbal communication, he or she will also be nonverbally communicating with you. In fact, researchers have consistently found that a good portion of what we communicate is communicated nonverbally and that non-verbal communication is extremely important in understanding the meaning of the message.

As a therapist I have been trained to look for inconsistencies between what a person is saying and how he or she is saying it. I was trained to view communication in terms of a metaphor: the content of a message is like the words to a song, whereas the emotional tone is like the music. When I listen to a client, I ask myself two questions. One, is the music accompanying the words? And two, are the person's comments consistent with the music?

These are two different questions. The first deals with the degree to which a person is emotionally present when he or she communicates. Is the speaker experiencing or present to what he or she is saying? Or does he or she seem to be reading a report?

I had a patient report a gruesome story. She was eleven years old when this incident occurred. Her drunken father came home furious one night. No one knew what set him off that night, but his rage escalated. Finally, after terrorizing them for hours, he murdered his wife and then tied up his two children. He then set fire to the house and committed suicide by blowing his brains out with a shotgun. My client and her brother were rescued by the fire department. She narrated this terrifying, traumatic experience in a very objective, detached manner. The pain was just too great for her to experience. The "music" wasn't there. After several months of therapy, she began to connect her emotions to the experience. Shortly thereafter her night terrors stopped. She began enjoying a full night of sleep.

The second issue addresses the content of the message. I ask myself, "Do the lyrics match the music? Is the subject being discussed consistent with the emotional energy in the speaker's behavior?" I once worked with a young man who was obviously very upset with his wife for hounding him about his lack of feelings for her. Yet what he said to her was 180 degrees out from this subject. He began complaining about the way she cleaned house instead of discussing what he didn't like about the way that he was being treated.

Offer to discuss your observation with your partner when a discrepancy arises in your own or your partner's behavior. These discussions are guaranteed to be of value to the relationship. When I point out discrepancies to my clients, I discover that most of the time they are functioning with little awareness of what is missing in their behavior. When you become aware of an incongruity in your behavior, this new awareness helps you change your behavior to more genuinely reflect your true position. *Becoming aware of the congruence of your verbal and nonverbal behavior helps you deliver your whole message. Delivering your whole message is critical if you are to have an intimate relationship with your partner.*

Speak in the First and Second Person

Being personal involves being vulnerable as you make contact with the person you are communicating to. In order to be personal, communicate by speaking in the first person ("I" statements) and the second person ("you" statements). Most of the time we communicate with "we" or "us" or "people feel this way or that way," which means that we are playing it safe by being general and vague, but we pay a price. We distance ourselves from contact, and we lose our connection, intimacy, vitality and passion. Take a risk! Take a stand and state what you want. "I want to be close to you," or "I want to spend more time with you," or "I don't want to please you right now." Such statements reveal who you are and what you want. Be authentic. You can only have a healthy relationship if it is based on who you really are and not some role you are playing to be accepted or liked or validated.

Discuss Specific Issues

Direct communication is best served if you strive to be as specific as possible when you are having a discussion regarding something you want or something you do not like. Try to avoid making statements like "I don't like our relationship!" or "You never listen to me." These statements are too global and too absolute to effectively communicate your position. Your partner will not know what you are talking about, and most likely he or she will respond defensively.

If you are specific with your partner, you have a better chance of getting what you want and enlisting his or her cooperation. Following are some examples of effective communication:

➠ "I don't like it when you interrupt me when I am talking. Please wait until I am finished, and then I will hear you out."

➠ "I don't like to have to reassemble the newspaper before I read it. When you are finished reading, I want you to refold the newspaper and arrange the sections."

➠ "I'm frustrated. It seems like you are not listening to me when I tell you I don't want to go and spend the afternoon watching football. I want you to hear what I am saying to you right now!"

➠ "I miss making love to you. I'd like to know how you really feel about making love to me!"

As you can see from these examples, the communicator is referencing the here-and-now in all of his or her remarks. This is called living in the moment. The more we live in the moment, the more present we are and the more personal and effective we can be as communicators.

Check Out Your Understanding

Most misunderstandings can be easily prevented if we quit assuming that we understand what our partners are communicating. This assumption can be deadly and has formed the basis for an entire approach to couples counseling. Couples are encouraged to take the time to assure that each understands what the other is saying. Couples are taught to paraphrase what they have heard. "I hear you saying _____ _____ (*fill in the blank*)." This gives their partners the opportunity to confirm or modify their understanding. Another technique couples are taught in this approach is to inquire about their partner's understanding of what they are saying. "Please share with me your understanding of what I've been talking about." This invitation for feedback helps you understand your partner's perception and theoretically improves communication.

While this technique has been touted in couples communication programs, its effectiveness has been questioned. The concern is that this approach reinforces emotional dependency because it emphasizes reciprocal communication: "I'll communicate in this manner, but you must do likewise." Participants are taught to paraphrase what they are hearing and then ask for a confirmation or revision. At times this can be helpful, but don't buy into the idea that your partner *must* cooperate with you. Remember, the most important thing you can do for your relationship is to work on yourself and be certain that you are functioning the way you want to function in your relationship. Do not demand that your partner does likewise. It's up to him or her to decide what kind of partner he or she wants to be, and you can rest assured that pressuring him or her will not facilitate that process.

While I encourage you to check out your understanding, it is equally if not more important for you to focus on how and what you are communicating. If you focus on what and how you are communicating, you will increase the likelihood of making a good connection with your partner.

Communicate as an Ally in a Positive Way

As you know, I have been encouraging you to tell your partner what you like and dislike. But there are many ways to say what you like and dislike. How you talk to your partner is every bit as important as what you are talking about. The best way to tell someone what you like or dislike is as an ally, as a best friend. In fact, studies of married couples by the Timberlawn Psychiatric Research Foundation have found that this element was prevalent in what they termed the highly competent marriages. They also found that when you make your spouse an equal partner and best friend, your children have the greatest chance of becoming psychologically healthy.

At times it will be difficult to treat your partner as your best friend. We all have demons that make it hard for us to believe that someone is genuinely interested in what we want or how we feel. But if you keep the following in mind, it might help you neutralize the effects of some of your demons.

As I mentioned earlier, I believe we all have the desire to cooperate with the life of the person we love. This means that we are interested in each other's personal desires. In fact, our strong desire to please often interferes with hearing our partner's displeasure or disappointment.

I recall an elderly couple, James and Mercy, with whom I worked for two years. The recurring theme in their relationship was her unhappiness and his difficulty in listening to her pain. James always wanted to ameliorate her discomfort. As we explored their interactions further, it became obvious that the thought he had displeased or failed Mercy created an unbearable pain. To avoid his pain he felt compelled to talk her out of the way she felt, or completely dismiss or discredit her feelings. Mercy concluded from his behavior that James really didn't care for her. But, in fact, the opposite was true. *He cared too much.* Once he became better at letting Mercy see what he was really feeling, she was able to better appreciate what he could offer her, rather than criticize him for what was missing.

Their problem could have been avoided if they had been able to approach one another as friends. Mercy could have said to James, "I know that you care about me. And yet when I talk to you about my disappointment, you have a very difficult time listening to me. I'm sure there must be a very good reason for that. Maybe we can talk about what happens to you in order for me to better understand you."[1]

Or James could have told Mercy, "I love you very much, and it is tremendously painful for me when I believe that I have disappointed you. It is so painful that I want to run away from what you are saying. I'm not sure I can bear the pain."

As you can see, a conversation like this starts from a position of mutual respect: "I am a good person and so are you. Therefore there must be a good reason we are having this difficulty." There is no blame, just self-disclosure and a search for what each can do to address the problem at hand. Their efforts are focused on finding a solution. Being solution-focused is an important element in approaching each other as an ally.

Do not be discouraged if you fall short of this goal. *Please remember, if you try to function as an ally and you are not successful, your efforts are not wasted.* The effects from trying to relate to your partner in this way are almost as positive and rewarding as being successful. Your intentions let your partner know that he or she is important to you.

The second element to being an ally is communicating what you want in a positive way. If you don't like something your

---

[1] *A truth that I have stumbled across in my practice is that if you are feeling misunderstood, it means that you are also misunderstanding. Therefore, the cure to this problem is to apply a bit of understanding to your partner, and in return you will be understood.*

READER/CUSTOMER CARE SURVEY

We care about your opinions! Please take a moment to fill out our online Reader Survey at **http://survey.hcibooks.com.** As a **"THANK YOU"** you will receive a **VALUABLE INSTANT COUPON** towards future book purchases as well as a **SPECIAL GIFT** available only online! Or, you may mail this card back to us and we will send you a copy of our exciting catalog with your valuable coupon inside.

(PLEASE PRINT IN ALL CAPS)

First Name		MI.		Last Name	

Address					

State		Zip			Email		City

1. Gender
- ❏ Female
- ❏ Male

2. Age
- ❏ 8 or younger
- ❏ 9-12
- ❏ 13-16
- ❏ 17-20
- ❏ 21-30
- ❏ 31+

3. Did you receive this book as a gift?
- ❏ Yes
- ❏ No

4. Annual Household Income
- ❏ under $25,000
- ❏ $25,000 - $34,999
- ❏ $35,000 - $49,999
- ❏ $50,000 - $74,999
- ❏ over $75,000

5. What are the ages of the children living in your house?
- ❏ 0 - 14
- ❏ 15+

6. Marital Status
- ❏ Single
- ❏ Married
- ❏ Divorced
- ❏ Widowed

7. How did you find out about the book?
(please choose one)
- ❏ Recommendation
- ❏ Store Display
- ❏ Online
- ❏ Catalog/Mailing
- ❏ Interview/Review

8. Where do you usually buy books?
(please choose one)
- ❏ Bookstore
- ❏ Online
- ❏ Book Club/Mail Order
- ❏ Price Club (Sam's Club, Costco's, etc.)
- ❏ Retail Store (Target, Wal-Mart, etc.)

9. What subject do you enjoy reading about the most?
(please choose one)
- ❏ Parenting/Family
- ❏ Relationships
- ❏ Recovery/Addictions
- ❏ Health/Nutrition
- ❏ Christianity
- ❏ Spirituality/Inspiration
- ❏ Business Self-help
- ❏ Women's Issues
- ❏ Sports

10. What attracts you most to a book?
(please choose one)
- ❏ Title
- ❏ Cover Design
- ❏ Author
- ❏ Content

TAPE IN MIDDLE; DO NOT STAPLE

BUSINESS REPLY MAIL
FIRST-CLASS MAIL PERMIT NO 45 DEERFIELD BEACH, FL

POSTAGE WILL BE PAID BY ADDRESSEE

Health Communications, Inc.
3201 SW 15th Street
Deerfield Beach FL 33442-9875

|..||...||..|..|..|..|..|..|..||||..|..|..|..|..||..|.||..|.|.|

FOLD HERE

Comments

CHAPTER 6

Understanding and Strengthening the Emotional Climate of Your Relationship

*W*e've got this gift of love, but love is like a precious plant. You can't just accept it and leave it in the cupboard or just think it's going to get on by itself. You've got to keep watering it. You've got to really look after it and nurture it.

—John Lennon (1969)

Colorless, odorless, tasteless: Whatever is being described doesn't sound too impressive, does it? Yet these three words describe oxygen. We don't spend a lot of time thinking about oxygen unless we're jammed in a crowded elevator or stuck 150 feet below the surface of the Pacific with an empty dive tank. Then we become very attentive to the life-giving qualities of oxygen.

Like oxygen, many of the most powerful influences in our lives are invisible and unnoticed. Think of gravity, electricity or sunlight. We cannot see these forces or touch them, yet their power over our lives is immense, their absence devastating. Emotions are among the invisible forces that are continuously shaping our existence.

Here is a striking example of the power of emotion. Shortly after World War II, babies were dying in inexplicable ways. These infants were not the victims of bombs or bullets. They were orphans fortunate enough to have survived the war. They were sheltered in orphanages where they were nourished with good food and kept warm and dry. Yet they kept dying. Physicians were baffled.

At that time the children were diagnosed as having "anaclitic depression." They were dying from lack of love.

Although it seemed that all of their basic physical needs were being met, staffing at the orphanages was limited and the babies were rarely held or cuddled. What we have learned from this sad natural experiment is that love, bonding and touching are not luxuries. They are also basic needs, as fundamental as food or water to human infants.

As adults we continue to be enormously influenced by emotions. The emotional atmosphere in our relationships is incredibly powerful in our lives. We fashion that climate from myriad interactions: the ways we treat each other, what we say and what we don't, the gestures we make and the ones we withhold, the secrets we share and those we keep. Our relationship climate is an amalgam of all of our attitudes and behaviors toward each other.

The climate in a relationship can range from therapeutic, healthy and loving to harmful and dysfunctional. If the climate in your relationship is therapeutic, you and your partner will thrive and flourish and further strengthen your partnership. If you are living in a dysfunctional emotional climate, problems become war zones, either hot or cold, and they weaken rather than support the relationship.

Most relationships can be classified somewhere between healthy and dysfunctional. Regardless of where your relationship falls, you will probably be able to identify both pluses and minuses in what occurs between you and your partner. If your relationship is in trouble, you will let yourself know that somehow, something important is missing from your life.

Sometimes the message is clear and conscious. You are not enjoying yourself in the relationship. It is a burden, and you don't look forward to time with your partner. At other times the message we send ourselves must be decoded. Here are some behaviors that signal a relationship problem. You feel depressed or angry most of the time. You work constantly. You drink or eat too much. You have affairs. You've become obsessed with your tennis game. These behaviors tell you something important is missing in your relationship.

This chapter is devoted to the attitudes and behaviors that generate healthy emotional climates. Consider your own particular situation and try to identify new elements that you would like to add to your relationship.

Setting and Respecting
Appropriate Boundaries

Psychological boundaries are extremely important in a relationship or family. A psychological boundary is exactly like a
border between countries, except it is a border between you and
the world. It delineates the "me" and the "not me" in much the
same way that a political boundary separates Canada from the
United States or Israel from the occupied territories.

Notice that the two examples I have used demonstrate radi-
cally different types of borders, one more open, the other
closed and rigid. Like these political borders, psychological
boundaries range on a continuum from rigid and inflexible to
porous and poorly defined. If your boundaries are chronically
fixed at either end of this spectrum, you are going to have difficulty in relationships.

Here is an example. Several years ago a new client named
Conrad came to see me, accompanied by his wife, Clarice, and
their three children. Conrad said he had come because everyone,
including his wife, was perpetually upset with him for no appar-
ent reason.

When I asked Clarice and the children to offer Conrad some
feedback regarding his behavior, they unanimously agreed that
once he made up his mind or set a rule there was no room for
discussion. It was his way or no way. Conrad had completely
rigid boundaries.

On the other hand, another client of mine named Catherine
complained bitterly, "My friends are constantly taking advantage
of me." Yet Catherine felt compelled to give anybody anything
they wanted. Her real problem was not her exploitive friends.

Her real problem was that she could not say "No." Her boundaries were as poorly defined as Conrad's were rigid.

Most of us have difficulty setting healthy boundaries. Some of us are autocratic like Conrad, and others are like Catherine and have trouble saying "No." The latter are often referred to as people pleasers or codependents. These individuals let others take advantage of them, they get lost in the problems or concerns of others, and they let spouses abuse them and children disrespect them.

So what is a healthy boundary? A healthy boundary is one that takes care of you, protects you and constrains you from acting in a way that will be harmful; it also reflects how you feel and what you want. A healthy boundary protects you from being hurt or abused and stops you from hurting or abusing someone you care about, but it also lets in the nourishment that you need. Healthy boundaries are clearly defined yet flexible enough for you to remain open to your desires, changing needs or new information. People are not static. We are in a constant state of flux. What you want today may be different from what you want tomorrow.

To a certain degree, boundaries are correlated with your need to join or separate from your partner. Most of us are usually better at one or the other.

Traditionally men are better at separating from relationships, while most women are better at joining. I believe that this gender difference develops when boys must break their psychological identity with mother by saying, "No. I'm not like you!" This early split from mother becomes a prototype in men's lives, meaning that it will always be easier for men to leave than join.

The early separation of boys and their mothers may also

explain why men have so much difficulty making commitments to relationships. It is not because we have cold feet, as some female psychologists have suggested. It is because we are skewed in the "No" direction. Once, when I was giving a lecture, one of the males in the audience was wearing a hat that read "BEFORE YOU EVEN ASK, THE ANSWER IS NO." I've never seen a woman wear a hat or T-shirt with that type of message.

Women say "Yes." They say "Yes" to their mothers, and they say "Yes" to life in general because of their biology, their ability to conceive life. Thus, the prototype in their lives is "Yes." Why is it that most of the people who suffer from co-dependency are women? I believe it is because women say "Yes," making them extremely vulnerable to codependent tendencies.

Be aware of these differences between men and women—the desire to join versus the desire to separate—because they potentially influence every one of our intimate relationships. Men can learn a lot from women and vice versa.

Typically we pick partners who will teach us how to develop the missing skills in our life. We need the other person to inspire us to become more whole, to develop aspects of ourselves that need improvement. In order to "hold on to ourselves," to grow up emotionally and become more self-supportive, we need to learn to set boundaries, to say "Yes" when it is appropriate (that is, when we want to), and to say "No" when it is appropriate (that is, when we don't want to).

The first step in setting a healthy boundary in your relationship is to clearly define what you want. Your personal desires or preferences will become your boundaries. "I don't like how you are talking to me," "I want you to touch me in a gentler way," "I don't want to make love tonight" and "I don't like how you are treating me" are all examples of setting boundaries.

The second step is to monitor your boundary to ensure that it reflects what you really want. You may revise the boundary at any time or any point. It is okay to say to your partner, "I said I wanted to be left alone right now, but as I said that to you I felt sad and empty. I'm not sure that's what I really want. I want to be close to you, but I don't want to be sexual tonight."

The third step is to respect your boundaries and your partner's boundaries. I've always had a hard time respecting my boundaries or the boundaries of others. I used to set a boundary by analyzing its reasonableness or by consulting my fears to see if my boundary was appropriate. Since I viewed almost any need on my part as unreasonable, and since fear permeated most of my interpersonal encounters, there wasn't much room left to set boundaries. Then about ten years ago, I heard Dr. Kempler say, *"When you are an adult the best reason for you to do something or not is because you WANT TO or DON'T WANT TO. There is no better reason to do something than because it is what you want to do."* This was a revolutionary concept to me, and it has helped me learn how to respect my boundaries and the boundaries of my partner.

If you set a boundary and then alter your position because you do not want a fight or because you are afraid of losing the relationship, you are not honoring your own integrity. You are either letting fear control your life, or you are letting some set of alien rules control your life. The culprit behind these crippling ideas is emotional dependency. If you let ideas influenced by emotional dependency run your life, you will feel that you are not in charge. You will feel like a victim in your relationships, always reacting and never letting your personal desires determine your behavior or your life.

I believe that it's a psychological axiom that *you will not be able to respect your partner's boundaries if you do not respect your own!* If you are able to respect your own boundaries, you will be better at respecting your partner when he or she says "No."

Staying Solution-Focused When You Encounter a Problem

Blaming creates a win/lose situation. It is harmful in a romantic relationship. Blame is characteristic of a dysfunctional relationship. When a couple in a healthy relationship confronts a problem, they tend to focus on the solution to the situation at hand and not get sidetracked by irrelevant issues like who's to blame. I refer to this process as being "solution-focused."

This skill is extremely important to a healthy relationship because even the best relationships encounter problems. Problems are a part of the basic human condition. Therefore, it is normal to experience relationship difficulties.

Working together to effectively solve problems takes a certain type of attitude. Here are its cornerstones. First, you must focus on what needs to be done about the problem. This means that you and your partner have to discuss your assessment of the situation and what corrective action each of you recommends. This is where your differences can be of great value. Because of your differences, you will each perceive unique aspects of the situation. These divergent perspectives can be extremely helpful because you will be able to glean valuable information that will help you develop a comprehensive approach to the problem.

The second step is to generate a plan of what must be done to address the problem or to prevent the problem from happening again. There must be consensus in order for you both to support the solution wholeheartedly. You must be on guard that you or your partner is not giving in for the sake of convenience or agreeing to something because he or she doesn't want "the hassle."

Once you have found a mutually agreeable solution, your next step will be to focus on the assets or resources you have to implement your solution. This will include a discussion of each person's ability to address the problem at hand. Please note that I said "ability," not what needs to be done. Remember our desire to contribute to the solution will be greater than our ability, and therefore you and/or your partner are likely to volunteer beyond your ability. *Acknowledging and respecting your limitations is extremely important in generating a reality-based solution to your common problems.*

The third step in your discussion involves taking responsibility for what you have been doing to contribute to the problem and then making a commitment about what you will do to solve the problem. It's important to note that this step involves taking responsibility for your behavior and making a personal commitment regarding what you will do to affect a solution. In a healthy relationship each person takes responsibility for his or her behavior. This does not include coaching your partner about what he or she should be responsible for or what changes you want him or her to make—a common mistake. Most of us have a tendency to focus on what our partner has done or what our partner should or should not do. Invariably this approach gets you sidetracked into an argument. Meddling is intrusive and typically leads to a "Don't tell me what to do" type of reaction. *Being in a relationship does not authorize you to tell your partner what he or she should or should not do.* Giving feedback to each other is only appropriate if it's invited or if a partner asked for permission to do so.

The last step of the solution-focused process is evaluation of your efforts. You both need to follow up on your commitments and monitor the solution to see if it is in fact doing what you hoped it would do. Experience is a great teacher. If you can both remain open to what your experience is telling you about your solution, you will be able to make appropriate modifications. For example, you may get what you thought you wanted only to decide that it is not what you really wanted after all. Changes are in order. You will have to modify your solution to integrate this new information.

A moving example of how this process works comes to mind. A couple, married for about five years, came to see me at the brink of divorce. In our first interview, Angela could hardly stop crying long enough to tell me about her pain. Walter seemed quite anxious about the serious trouble in the marriage, but like many men, he responded aggressively to his wife's accusations.

The problem they were having related to the difficulty Walter had in setting a boundary between his mother and his nuclear family. His mother was a practicing alcoholic. She was extremely negative and constantly criticized Angela during visits to their home. After trying hard for several months to make the relationship with her mother-in-law work, Angela gave up.

She felt frustrated with Walter's lack of support. Walter didn't like his mother's rudeness either, and he would intermittently challenge her and forbid her to visit. Then, invariably, he would soften and invite her back to their house.

Walter's problem in maintaining a boundary with his mother stemmed from assuming responsibility for her feelings. His father had abandoned the family when Walter was six years old, and Walter stepped into the void, as children do. He believed he should take care of his mother, a feeling that continued into adulthood. Now he is reluctant to tell his mother she cannot visit because he knows she would be saddened by not seeing her grandson.

I confronted Walter quite strongly about his inability to set appropriate boundaries with his mother. I pointed out that his family was now his priority, not his mother. Walter was quick to see the value of this principle, and he turned to his wife in tears and apologized for not being a better husband.

The following week Walter and Angela reported that they were much closer to each other and that a long-gone tenderness had been rekindled. In this second session we began discussing the nuts and bolts of the situation. I delineated Walter's dilemma: He didn't know how to please both his wife and his mother. Then I encouraged the couple to discuss what each of them could do to resolve this problem. Walter started to look at his difficulty in setting boundaries with his mother, and Angela focused on how to stay at her husband's side even though he was not able to be at her side.

You do to your partner what you accuse him of doing to you. Angela had correctly complained of being abandoned, but she had also abandoned Walter by criticizing him when they discussed the issue. In the beginning, offering support to Walter was impossible for Angela, as it is for most people in her situation, but eventually she was able to understand that Walter truly wanted to be a good husband. He just didn't know how.

A large part of my work with couples is to help partners learn how to be a part of the solution rather than fall into a destructive tit-for-tat dynamic. Remember you can only be a part of the solution if you stop blaming and instead focus on what needs to be done to find a solution to the problem at hand. A helpful tool can be to identify and emphasize the positive intentions in your partner's behavior rather than criticizing him or her.

Respect and Appreciate Individual Differences, and That Doesn't Mean Paying Lip Service to Those Differences

Respecting the differences between you and your partner begins with appreciating what the differences are and then learning the value of these differences. I have helped many couples turn around marriages filled with conflict by helping them see their differences and then realize the value of these differences.

One model of personality types I use to help couples appreciate their differences is a model that was originally developed by Carl Jung and later revised by Myers and Briggs.

Read the following descriptions and ask yourself where you fall along each of these dimensions. Ask your partner to do the same, and then sit down and compare your ratings and read the following sections. If you are honest with yourself, it should help you to appreciate and value your differences.

EXTROVERTED AND INTROVERTED TYPES

Extroverts are externally focused. When they encounter a problem, they want to talk things through immediately. Introverts look within themselves for information. They are focused internally and need a certain degree of psychological space in a relationship. When introverts have a problem, they sit and think before talking about it.

If a couple is not aware of these differences, they can end up in a terrible conflict. The extrovert will attack the introvert and say something like, "You never want to deal with any of the problems in the relationship." In reality, the introvert simply deals with problems in a different way. It's not a question of wanting or not wanting to deal with the problem. It's a question of style. Personality style determines how he or she will address the problem.

In a healthy relationship an extrovert and an introvert can enjoy a balance between inner and outer worlds. On the one hand, the extrovert will expose the introvert to the outer world and the value of establishing a social network. On the other hand, the introvert will introduce the extrovert to the value of spending time alone and the value of introspection.

When there are problems in the relationship, the extrovert will want to talk the matter through to discover how they both feel or think about the situation. The introvert will need to do the opposite. He or she will need to become quiet to find himself or herself, before feeling ready to discuss the matter further.

Intuitive and Sensing Types

Intuitive types look at the future and at possibilities, while sensing types are more focused on the pragmatics of the "here and now." Therefore, intuitive and sensing types can help each other enjoy both the dreams and realities of life. The intuitive type can introduce novel solutions to problems and encourage the sensing type to experiment and try new things, while the sensing type can help keep the couple grounded in reality and put the intuitive person's ideas into action.

However, if these differences are not recognized and respected, they can create problems. For example, when an intuitive type and a sensing type argue, they often run into trouble because they are talking about different things. The intuitive person will be angry and upset about the implied meaning of what was said, while the sensing type will be upset because the intuitive person will not get the facts straight. You'll often hear a sensing type say, "What I said to you was, I don't want to do *that*. It's not that I don't want to be with you." The intuitive partner reads something negative between the lines like, "You really don't want to be with me, so why don't you just come out and tell me that you don't?"

A second set of problems occurs when there is too great a gap between dreams and reality, or between the lure of the future and the joys of the present. The intuitive type will be focused on the possibilities that the future offers, while the sensing type will be focused on the here and now. When this happens the intuitive type may feel restricted by the reality framework of the sensing type. If the intuitive type interprets the sensing type's motivation negatively, he or she may conclude that the sensing type is doing this out of a desire to control. When this kind of interpretation is made, a power struggle is inevitable. *What the intuitive person needs to remember is that the sensing type behaves this way because of who he or she is, and not because of a need to control. What the sensing type needs to remember is to not take the intuitive's discussion of future possibilities literally.* Talking about the possibilities is not tantamount to wanting to take action, which is what the sensing type expects.

A third set of problems occurs when the intuitive type doesn't take the sensing type's words literally and, therefore, not seriously. Sensing types are going to be very concrete and clear about what they want. They are not going to be vague and abstract, in the manner of the intuitive type. Therefore, what they say is what they want. It is not a discussion of possibilities.

FEELING AND THINKING TYPES

Feeling types make decisions based on a consideration of how all the concerned parties will feel about it. Thinking types are logical and systematic in decision making. When a thinking type and a feeling type come together, their differences can help them make well-rounded decisions, based on an overview of both sides of the proverbial coin. The feeling type will introduce important subjective considerations, whereas the thinking type will present more logical or objective concerns. Another potential benefit of their differences is that the feeling type can help the thinking type get in touch with and respect his or her own feelings, while the thinking type can help the feeling type toughen up in his or her dealings with the outer world, when necessary.

Problems will arise, however, if the thinking type devalues the feeling type's need to consider the feelings of other people. When this happens you will often hear the thinking type argue that the feeling type is behaving irrationally. In reality, the feeling type is irrational. Remember, the feeling type is concerned with the emotional world, which is not logical. However, this does not imply that the feeling type's perspective is any less valid or valuable than the thinking type's perspective. It's not! Both perspectives have value and can make a significant contribution to a decision.

The thinker's tendency to criticize, or the feeling type's tendency to take criticism personally, is also a difference that may create difficulties. What usually happens when the thinking type is critical is that the feeling type will overtly express his or her hurt feelings. In reaction, the thinking type may withdraw into an aloof and impersonal analysis of the situation, believing that this is the best way to help when, in fact, it exacerbates the hurt of the partner. One does not suppress flames with buckets of gasoline! When a couple has this kind of problem, they usually end up caught in a very negative cycle and need to seek professional help to interrupt and change the pattern.

Judging and Perceiving Types

Judging types impose organization and structure on their environments. Perceiving types are spontaneous, flexible and adaptable, and they value freedom. They see change as a challenge and, therefore, welcome it into their lives. At its best, a relationship with the judging/perceiving combination can have a healthy balance between work and play, decisiveness and openness, and spontaneity and organization. If the partners value their differences, they will appreciate the perceiving type's need to be sure that all the necessary information goes into their decision, while the judging type will contribute a plan of action to implement the results of that decision.

When things go wrong between a couple who have this combination of types, it's usually because they misunderstand and, therefore, disrespect their differences. For example, the judging type's need to control and organize everything and everybody may collide with the perceiving type's need to have freedom in order to remain open and spontaneous. The perceiving type may end up feeling boxed in or too restricted by the judging type's plans and decisions. Conversely, the judging type may feel anxious until he or she knows a decision has been made. When judging types feel anxious, they usually increase their efforts to control. This is met by increased efforts for independence on the part of the perceiving type. When this happens, the judging type ends up pursuing the perceiving type, and they become hopelessly engaged in a negative, vicious cycle.

You may be wondering how partners can disengage themselves from these problems, or from any of the style-combination problems that have been discussed. To date, the best solution I have found is based on the principle that an individual can have any set of rules he or she wants for his or her own behavior, but you cannot expect other people to comply with your rules. **My rules are fine for me, but I do not have the right to expect you to live by them.** The best thing about a rule like this is that it works both ways. Thus, your partner does not have the right to impose his or her rules on you either. This attitude creates the freedom and space for you to live together in a respectful and loving way. There has to be room enough for both of you in the relationship. If the relationship is skewed in one direction or the other, it will not flourish and thrive. It will become oppressive, and you will either feel controlled or become controlling.

Every combination of personality types has its assets and liabilities. In order for us to improve our relationships and have a clear understanding of what is happening between us, and what assets we can use to help solve our problems, we need to understand and respect the differences in our personality styles.

There will be room in the relationship for how I feel and what

I want, and how you feel and what you want. Our differences are appreciated and welcomed.

Encourage Each Other to Live Life from a Foundation of Personal Authenticity

About twenty years ago, assertiveness training hit the mental health market. Its proponents encouraged people to set appropriate boundaries and to say "No" effectively. Saying "No" is still an extremely important interpersonal skill, but today many therapists are helping people with an equally important skill: asking for what they want. As a therapist, I have found that it's even more difficult for people to ask for what they want than to say "No."

This is where we need help the most. As I have written in several places in this book, we all have difficulty telling each other what we want. Even the person who seems to be taking care of his "self" or her "self" well will have areas in his or her life where he or she is not.

In a healthy relationship, honest language forms the cornerstone for all interactions, and hopefully there will be support and encouragement to function from a personal foundation that is based on what you want, what you don't want and what you feel. Even if your partner is not supportive of your attempts to be more personal and authentic, you need to keep in mind that you are doing this for your sake, not for his or her validation or support.

Remember Dr. Kempler's idea that "When you are an adult, the best reasons you can have for doing something or not doing something is because you WANT to do it or you don't WANT to."

Inspiration to live your life with such passion comes from knowing yourself and your true desires. Each partner has the responsibility for knowing and expressing his or her own needs. When a couple is committed to integrity in their lives, they will be encouraging and supportive in their partner's quest for authenticity.

For example, you can encourage this spirit in your partner by keeping constant vigilance over your own integrity, and by not accepting anything from your partner that is not freely given. Do not accept your partner selling out his or her own personal needs or desires. Such a sacrifice will not be to your advantage in the long run. It can only harm and weaken the integrity of your relationship.

Integrity is not a choice. It is a necessary condition for a healthy relationship and therefore must be safeguarded and encouraged at all times. In fact, couples should settle for nothing less.

CHAPTER 7

Adjustments at Close Range: Seven Surefire Ways to Solve Problems

I want relations which are not purely personal, based on purely personal qualities; but relations based upon some unanimous accord in truth or belief, and a harmony of purpose, rather than of personality. I am weary of personality. . . . Let us be easy and impersonal, not forever fingering over our own souls, and the souls of our acquaintances, but trying to create a new life, a new common life, a new complete tree of life from the roots that are within us.

—D. H. LAWRENCE (1915)

Our concern now shifts to solving typical problems between partners: what to do when you and your partner are struggling with an issue and getting nowhere; what to do when you hit an impasse; how to free up marital gridlock; how to apply the ideas presented in this book during the heat of battle. I refer to this as "making adjustments at close range."

Before we discuss these suggestions, I want to let you know where I stand on using formulas to solve your relationship problems. I am not in favor of a step-by-step approach to problem-solving because no program is flexible enough to be responsive to the unique challenges couples face in their relationships. Nowhere is there a relationship exactly like yours and your partner's. I am not saying, however, that you cannot benefit from certain ideas. You can, and therefore I will present you with seven suggestions that may be helpful when you hit gridlock. Use one or all of these suggestions whenever you and your partner hit a bump on the road of life. These suggestions are your emergency backup system and should be applied whenever the wheels seem to be coming off. Keep what works, and shelve the rest because they may be relevant on a different day or in dealing with a different situation or issue.

GIVE UP BEING RIGHT
OR RIGHTEOUS.

KEY ELEMENTS: Pride and righteousness may be contributing to the impasse and interfering with finding a solution to the problem between you and your partner.

My good friend often says to me when he is struggling with a marital problem, "I have to remind myself, 'Do I want to be right or be happy?'" My friend's dilemma points us toward an important perspective if you want to remove a major source of marital gridlock—false pride. False pride demands that we must be right all the time. It prevents us from making amends for inappropriate behavior, it contributes to endless quarrels about who is right and who is wrong, and it obstructs finding a workable solution to problems. False pride is dangerous when it comes to making a relationship work.

Why do I list this as the first item you need to consider as a way out of marital gridlock? For the majority of couples who are stuck in their relationships, needing to be right or acting righteous is a major source of their difficulty. Let's look at how this contributes to marital problems.

First, when you think you are right it means that someone else is wrong. This polarizes you and your partner. No solution can be found when you and your partner are polarized. As I explained earlier, this is linear thinking and it is not very helpful when trying to make adjustments at close range.

When you and your partner are polarized, respect for differences is impossible because you are unable to see any value in your partner's position. You have difficulty understanding his or her position, and being polarized blocks your ability to think creatively. You become rigid and pedantic, which ultimately impairs your problem-solving abilities.

Instead of focusing on who is right or wrong, or who is to blame, remember that it is what you *and* your partner are doing that is creating a problem. It is not what you *or* your partner is doing; both of you are contributing to the gridlock. This perspective can help you move beyond polarizing. It can help you refocus.

You may be asking yourself, "Where should I put my focus?" "How can I apply this knowledge to create a desirable change in my relationship?" The answer is that you need to focus on what you need to do to change your behavior. Remember: If either you or your partner begins to change, the relationship will change too. It doesn't matter who changes first! Sidestep the chicken-or-egg controversy and instead focus on finding a solution. If you can't, it may be that your false pride is getting in the way.

If it is more important for you to be right than to find a solution to your marital gridlock, then face the fact that this is where you are stuck, this is your limitation as a person. It has been my experience that when you declare your position, change may be possible. So make some outrageous declarations about needing to be right all the time. Admit that no matter what the cost to your life and your relationship, you need to be right. Then hope your partner picks up this book, turns to this section, and is open to this idea: the impasse is not going to be ameliorated by you. You're allowing your false pride to keep you from growing up and becoming an adult.

Now I know some of you may be thinking, "Dr. Berger is an arrogant bastard. He doesn't know my situation. I really am right. My husband was wrong to embarrass me in public (or whatever your partner has done). He should apologize, and I am not going to forgive him until he does."

I am not saying that your partner isn't contributing to the problem. I am certain he or she is, but that is his or her problem. Not yours! You can't do anything about his or her immature behavior, but you can do something about your behavior if you are willing to lay down your false pride and righteousness.

Take the woman who was embarrassed by her husband, for example. Her husband made some inappropriate comments in front of dinner guests about the size of her ass. She quickly responded that there was simply more of her for him to love. She neutralized his inappropriate comment with her sense of humor.

Now I am not advocating that you always use humor or sarcasm to deal with a situation, but at times humor and sarcasm may be the best antidote to your partner's inappropriate behavior. One suggestion I can offer if you are struggling is to search for the opposite behavior of what you typically do. If you are docile, try to be assertive. If you are aggressive, try to be consoling and understanding. If you are serious, lighten up. If you are indirect, be direct. If you are demanding, be understanding. Experiment and try the opposite. It might help.

SEARCH FOR THE PERSONAL GROWTH LESSON IN THE IMPASSE.

KEY ELEMENTS: Searching for the personal growth lesson in the marital gridlock will help you focus on what you can do to deal with the situation, rather than focusing on your partner.

Every impasse you encounter, every conflict you have trouble resolving, every resentment you harbor, every ongoing problem you have in your relationship, reflects your level of personal development. If you investigate these situations when you run into difficulty you will be rewarded with an opportunity for personal growth.

Whenever we reach an impasse in our relationship, it indicates that we are arrested at some stage of our personal development. As I stated earlier, I believe a deep wisdom helps influence our selection of partners. We pick partners with whom we are going to have a certain kind of therapeutic trouble. We choose partners with whom an issue will arise that will provide us an opportunity to take the next step in our emotional maturity. For instance, I am currently working with a man whose partner is frustrating him. He is used to getting his own way through intimidation. He is a big man, very aggressive, and he uses his size and assertiveness to bully people to submit to his will. The woman he dates typically caves in to these tactics, but eventually she builds up resentment and explodes. After several months of working on how to hold on to herself and set clearer boundaries with him, she stopped giving in to his bully tactics and no longer felt controlled.

This created quite a dilemma for him. If he wanted to continue with the relationship, he needed to grow up and develop a different way of dealing with her. Instead of calling her names, verbally threatening her or yelling at her, he had to learn how to respectfully deal with another person.

The thing about these dilemmas that arise in our relationships is that there are always two choices. He can change, or he can leave and run away. But he can never really run away because he will re-create the same problem in his next relationship, until he finally holds still long enough to learn the lesson, to grow up, and learn a better way of dealing with his frustration and need to control.

If you are at an impasse, remember that it holds the information you need to discover your personal lesson. Every situation you are struggling with tells you simultaneously where you are stuck in your personal development and what you need to do to grow up. Take the preceding example, for instance. The man in this situation was stuck at the emotional age where he bullies by using his size or force to get his way. He was stuck at a very early stage of emotional development. The relationship with his girl-friend provided him with an opportunity to grow up and find a more mature way of dealing with his frustration. The problem is that often people do not understand it is their underlying wisdom that chooses their partner. Therefore, they do not search for the lesson inherent in the struggle.

TAKE RESPONSIBILITY FOR WHAT YOU ARE DOING THAT CONTRIBUTES TO THE IMPASSE, WHETHER OR NOT YOUR PARTNER DOES LIKEWISE.

KEY ELEMENTS: Be focused on the solution: This is the only thing that you can control. Let go of the rest.

The approach I encourage you to adopt whenever you confront a problem or impasse in your relationship, regardless of its nature, is "I am a part of this problem, and therefore I can be a part of the solution." Understanding and accepting responsibility for your part of the problem is essential to finding more solid ground from which to obtain a useful perspective that will help you find a solution.

Remember, everything that happens in relationships is bilaterally determined, which means that both you and your partner mutually contribute to the situation. Whatever the problem—depression, anxiety, an eating disorder, alcoholism, other drug addictions, sexual acting out, anxiety—it concerns both you and your partner. No matter when or where the problem originated—before the onset of the relationship, inside the relationship, outside the relationship—if the problem persists, it concerns both you and your partner.

Now here's the hard part. Even though you and your partner are both contributing to the impasse, you need to forget about trying to understand or clean up your partner's side of the street. Worry about keeping your side of the street clean. You have the best chance of contributing to finding a solution to the problem if you focus on your behavior, rather than focusing on your partner's behavior. Therefore, **an important step in breaking free from gridlock is total acceptance of your responsibility for your behavior and complete accountability for your actions**.

At times, identifying your responsibility may not be easy, especially if your partner has a high-profile problem like alcoholism, sex addiction, anger or verbally abusive behavior. Usually we can clearly see what their problem is because it is obvious, but I am certain if you look closely and honestly at your behavior you will find your contributions too, even though they may be subtle. Sometimes you may need the help of a good therapist or a well-functioning Alanon or AA meeting (Alanon is a nonprofit organization to help the spouse, relative or significant other of a person who is suffering from alcoholism) to help you develop insight into your behaviors that contribute to the problem.

Here's a good application of what I have been discussing. Partners of people who have problems like alcoholism or other drug addictions find that their contribution to the problem is what we refer to as "enabling." Enabling manifests in many ways; here are a few of the more common ones:

⟶ **Making excuses for the person.** Mary would often call John's employer and say, "John isn't able to come to work today because he is sick," when in fact John was hungover. I am certain that Mary believed she was supporting her husband by calling in sick for him, but actually she was enabling John's alcohol problem. When she called John's employer, John didn't have to face the personal discomfort he would have experienced had he called his employer and lied. Mary not only protected him from taking responsibility for his behavior, she ensured that he would keep drinking.

➡ **Minimizing the damages of the person's behavior.**
I remember working with a mother and her three adult children. Her daughter was quite upset because of the excuses her mother had made for her father's drunken abusive behavior during her childhood. Many nights he came home drunk and summoned all three children from bed to line up for a fifteen-minute reprimand. Then he would suddenly send them off to bed. Needless to say, this terrified and traumatized the children. They seldom had a restful night's sleep because of the anxiety they experienced at bedtime, fearing that this night would bring another ordeal with their father. The mother's fear stopped her from intervening and objecting to her husband's drunken, bizarre and abusive behavior. She was afraid to challenge him lest he become angry or violent toward her. As an adult, the woman's daughter understood that it would have been dangerous for her mother to confront her father, but she couldn't under-stand why her mother wouldn't face how damaging and traumatizing this experience was for her. Her mother adamantly denied and minimized any deleterious effects of this early morning ordeal.

⟶ **Internalizing the problem rather than confronting
your partner.** This is another common way that people
enable their partners. Instead of confronting their
partners about his or her inappropriate behavior, they
internalize it and blame themselves. This keeps the heat
off of their partner by swallowing it whole. People who
use this tactic are also afraid of conflict. So instead of
taking a risk and discussing a difficult subject, they do to
themselves what they would like to do to their partner—
they turn their anger toward themselves. They belittle or
condemn their own behavior. They do unto themselves
what they dare not do to their partner.

⟶ **Falsely agreeing with your partner because you are
afraid of your partner's reaction.** This is the "emperor's
new clothes" dynamic. Remember everyone was afraid to
tell the ruthless emperor that he was prancing around in
his underwear because of his anger? The emperor's false
pride and arrogance made him believe that he was wearing a wonderful new outfit, when in fact he was in his
underwear. This dynamic happens all the time in relationships. We call it "pseudo-mutuality." A couple or
husband and wife act like they agree about a situation,
but the truth is they really don't. Differences are forced
underground because of a rule that demands agreement
on everything.

I believe that all of the ways a person contributes to the difficulties in a relationship are ultimately caused by emotional
dependency. Emotional dependency destroys your authenticity

and integrity, keeping you from objecting to inappropriate behavior and openly discussing your differences. It silences you. You do not express your needs and wants or your outrage about an injustice. You don't address the problem because you are afraid your partner is going to leave you.

I urge you to look at what keeps you from showing your authentic self to your partner. Lack of authenticity undermines the relationship. By identifying your contribution to the problem, you are well on the way to becoming a part of the solution and altering destructive patterns of behavior.

STEP 4:

SEARCH FOR A SOLUTION TO YOUR PROBLEMS THAT REPRESENTS AND RESPECTS THE PERSONAL DESIRES OF BOTH OF YOU AND YOUR PARTNER AND IS DIFFERENT FROM WHAT YOU HAVE TRIED IN THE PAST.

KEY ELEMENTS: Vigilance against submission and a commitment to find a win/win negotiation.

Research on what constitutes healthy communication in relationships consistently finds that when difficulties are encountered, healthy functioning couples focus on finding a solution, rather than getting lost in the blame game. Therefore, when you hit an impasse, look toward finding a mutually satisfying solution that respects the wishes or desires of both you and your partner. Remember, blame is irrelevant. It doesn't matter who's to blame. The important issue is finding a workable, mutually acceptable solution. Emphasize the solution, not the problem, and be open and willing to consider any possibility.

I suggest beginning your search for a solution by brainstorming. Consider any and all suggestions or proposals that might help you resolve the current issue or prevent this problem in the future. The more personal your suggestions, the better they are. Don't be modest. Take a risk and ask for what you want, don't censor anything. It is only by being honest with your partner about what is important that you will be able to begin the process of discovering a mutually satisfying solution. If you have trouble identifying what you want, then talk about your difficulty in identifying what you want. An exercise that might help is for you to search for your most outrageous wishes by imagining that you have been granted a wish. What would you wish for? What is most important to you at this time in your life? Your answers to these questions may help you identify what you want but don't dare request.

Expressing the essence of your personal desire is critical to this process because the goal here is to craft a solution that respects what is important to both of you. If you are reluctant to share your personal desires, then share that. But remember that it is not up to your partner to make you feel safe before you become vulnerable. It is up to you to provide the emotional support you need when you stand up for what is important to you.

Once you offer a clear and direct statement of what is important to you, encourage your partner to do likewise. This step is important because it is necessary for you and your partner to be clear about what you want before beginning negotiations.

After you both make your positions clear, begin discussing ideas for a solution that honors and respects both of your needs. The goal now is to find a solution that is mutually satisfying. The spirit of this discussion is best set by thinking of your relationship as your first child. Use this image to help you focus on being respectful and attentive to the welfare of this precious child during any and all discussions, especially when addressing a heated topic.

A suggestion I have offered couples to maintain respect is to begin your negotiations and discussions with a win/win mentality. Imagine yourself as an ambassador who, at the same time, is representing your own personal interests and guarding against your partner's submission to your will. You do not want your partner to give in because whatever you decide wouldn't be mutually acceptable. As Dr. Kempler has stated, "Love is not determined by a plan or a commitment, but rather is the result of how you interact with each other."

This type of attitude guarantees that you are not going to allow a solution that compromises either your needs or your partner's. Both of you must keep a constant vigil, guarding against any kind of submission, compliance or dominance. Anything less than willful agreement will undermine your efforts to find a win/win solution.

Remember, for this approach to be effective, stay focused on what you want. If the two of you are at an impasse and you cannot discover a mutually satisfying solution, take a time-out. Agree to discuss the problem later, but make sure that you are specific about when you are going to revisit the issue because "later" is too ambiguous. Taking a break from the action can open up new possibilities that neither of you have previously considered.

If you are still stuck after the time-out, then the next best solution to a win/win is a no-deal. In a no-deal solution you agree that you cannot agree. If a no-deal solution is not acceptable, then you need to consult a professional.

You must be willing to go to any lengths to find a mutually agreeable solution. Total commitment is essential. Halfhearted attempts are worse than telling your partner that you are not interested in dealing with the problem. Ensure that when you reach out to your partner, you are acting as an ally who is willing to do whatever is necessary to find a solution.

ENSURE THAT YOU TRULY UNDERSTAND THE SOLUTION AND ITS IMPLICATIONS.

KEY ELEMENTS: Check out your understanding with your partner. Take nothing for granted.

After you think you have found a mutually acceptable solution, you need to check out your understanding of the agreement. (Remember, understanding each other is nearly impossible!) Guard against misunderstandings. Misunderstandings are frustrating, and they can hurt even the most well-intentioned negotiations.

Checking out your understanding with each other can go a long way to preventing a misunderstanding. Here are some phrases you can use to achieve a clear understanding:

➧ "What I understand you're saying is _____
_____
_____
_____" (*fill in the blank*).

➧ "What the solution means to me is _____
_____
_____
_____. Is this what it means to you?"

➧ "I have agreed to do _____
_____
_____
(this or that). My understanding of what you have
agreed to do is _____
_____
_____."

The goal here is to ensure that you have a true understanding.
I urge you to go to great lengths in establishing a sound level of
understanding. Nothing is more frustrating than walking away
from the negotiating table thinking you have agreed upon a solution and discovering a day or two later that your solution was
based on a false assumption. Frustration from this source is
unnecessary and can be prevented by regularly taking this step.
So I urge you to check out what you believe to be true.

STEP 6:

MONITOR THE SOLUTION AND MAKE ADJUSTMENTS IF NECESSARY.

KEY ELEMENTS: Discuss the effects of the solution. If you want something you are not getting, let your partner know. He or she cannot read your mind. Be proactive. Show your concern for your partner by investigating how he or she feels about the solution. Strive to respect differences.

Now that you have developed a mutually agreed-upon solution and ensured your understanding of the plan, you must monitor the solution to see if it is in fact solving the problem it was intended to address. Keep an open channel between you and your partner. Discuss your reactions openly and honestly. If you are dissatisfied with some aspect or implementation of the solution, talk to your partner about how you would like it to be. Remember, he or she is unable to read your mind.

I urge you to utilize a positive approach when you are revising your plan. Always keep in mind that your partner is interested in pleasing you while trying to keep his or her own individuality or integrity.

Be flexible. People change what was important yesterday may be unimportant or less important today, and what was insignificant yesterday may be earth-shattering today. Be responsive to such changes in yourself and in your partner. Don't get caught up in inflexible and rigid rules. The most important result is that you and your partner feel that your wishes or desires are recognized and respected. Create room enough for two in your relationship.

I also encourage you to ask your partner how the solution is working for him or her. This step is especially critical if your partner has difficulty telling you what he or she wants. Your invitation can create just the opportunity to help your partner begin voicing dissatisfactions.

If you decide to ask your partner to discuss how he or she feels, be sincere. Don't fool yourself into thinking that you can hide unpopular feelings. Insincerity is obvious in one's body language. You can't mask feelings!

If you are insincere, you will sabotage your efforts to create a better relationship. Believe it or not, it is actually better to say "I am not interested" than to pretend.

And, finally, I would like you to check out with your partner how you are fulfilling your end of the agreement. This is often a difficult move because you are opening yourself up to criticism. However, in my opinion it is worth the risk.

Don't ask unless you really want to know. Once you ask, your partner has every right to share with you his or her perspective. Asking is not a maneuver intended to evoke appreciation, approval or validation. It is a quest for information and feedback as to how you are keeping your agreement. This feedback can help you decide if you need to make some adjustments or change some aspect of your behavior. Lastly, I warn you, don't expect your partner to ask you the same question. He or she may not, and that's okay.

APPRECIATE YOUR PARTNER'S EFFORTS AT RESOLUTION, ESPECIALLY WHEN THEY ARE UNSUCCESSFUL!

KEY ELEMENTS: Recognize and appreciate your partner's desire to improve the relationship and please you. Look for the positive intention in all of your partner's behavior.

This is the final suggestion I have, and it may be the most crucial. Most of us are far too critical and negative. We seldom acknowledge or express our appreciation to each other.

Expectations make it difficult for us to see how a person may be attempting to cooperate or please us. We all have a mind-set about what the expression of love should be. These ideas make it difficult to see our partners for who they really are. For instance, I've heard several exasperated clients state, "If I wanted my partner to know that I loved him I'd _____

_____ (*fill in the blank*).
Why doesn't he do the same for me?" The answer is simple: **You are not your partner. You do many things differently, and you express love differently.**

Just because we don't see our partner's desire to please us or cooperate with us doesn't mean that he or she doesn't want to. It simply means that we don't see it.

Let me provide you with two examples that illustrate a failure to see each other's desire to cooperate. In one, Fran was unhappy with Eric for how he addressed their son Adam's behavior at a soccer game. She had thought Adam was too aggressive and asked Eric to talk with him about it. Eric told Adam that what he had done was unnecessary, but he also told him he was proud of Adam's two goals.

When Fran approached Eric, she started the conversation by saying, "Eric, I thought you were going to reprimand Adam, but what you did was encourage him. I'm really upset that you didn't address his inappropriate behavior at the soccer game." Eric became immediately defensive and angry and attacked Fran for "always micromanaging his relationship with Adam." There was some truth to what Eric was saying, but what he didn't talk about was how difficult it was for him when Fran was not pleased with his behavior. He didn't deliver his entire message, so Fran was unable to understand what he was feeling.

From this example, you can see that a partner like Eric becomes angry when he hears he has disappointed his partner. It doesn't necessarily indicate that he doesn't care. In fact, I have often found that it means that he cares too much and cannot stand hearing that he or she has frustrated the most important person in his or her life.

Another common situation is a silent response. I have often seen that when a person falls silent in response to a difficult subject being discussed it doesn't mean that he or she is not committed to the relationship. Sometimes a person falls silent because he or she doesn't want to say something that may hurt the person they care about. In other words, many behaviors that may at first glance seem to indicate a lack of interest or commitment in a relationship really occur because the relationship is too important and therefore the person is knocked off balance.

This perspective has been referred to as "searching for the positive intention in your partner's behavior." Even when you don't see it, there likely exists a positive intention to your partner's behavior. This positive intention is likely to be present in those behaviors that are the most obnoxious or frustrating to you. One way of bringing positive intention into the foreground is to say something to your partner like, "I imagine you have good intentions here [referring to whatever situation the person has been struggling with], but I am unable to identify them. Can you tell me what your behavior is saying to me?" Sometimes this will nudge the discussion in a productive direction.

Dr. Gottman calls this a "soft start-up." Research has shown that it is easier to start off a conversation in a good way than repair an interaction that has started off on the wrong foot. So do your best to get off to a good start. It can help immensely when you are trying to solve a stubborn problem.

Now that we've covered each of my seven suggestions for adjustments at close range, I will illustrate their application in three real-life situations.

Greg and Diane: *Fighting Fair*

*T*he first scenario takes place in the home of Greg and Diane. They have been married for four and a half years. The verbal abuse in the relationship has been increasing over the past year in both its intensity and frequency. Greg is more verbally abusive than Diane, but on several occasions she has taken her shots too. Diane doesn't want to split up the marriage. Her preference would be to work things out with Greg. After several days of struggling with how to approach Greg, she decides to take the following tack.

Diane: "I have been feeling very sad about our relationship. We have been unkind and . . ." (Here Diane is attempting to approach Greg with the idea that they have a problem.)

Greg: "But it's not always my fault. You've been pretty rotten to me, too." (When a relationship has been riddled with blame, a partner will hear blame even though it is not present.)

Diane: "Honey, I am not blaming you for what has happened. I don't like how I have acted either. But what concerns me most is what has been happening between us. I want to find a way to stop the disrespectful and abusive behavior on both of our parts." (Diane centers herself and reassures Greg that she is not blaming him, but rather searching for a solution.)

Greg: (Greg is still having some difficulty believing the true purpose of Diane's intentions and needs to share his difficulty with Diane. She isn't able to read his mind.) "It's really hard for me to believe that you are not blaming me."

Diane: "I understand it is difficult for you to believe me. I have often blamed you in the past. I want you to know that I'll do whatever is necessary to convince you. I don't want to get lost in who's to blame. My sole concern is making our relationship better. Let's brainstorm some ideas that might help. Then we can sort through them together." (Diane continues to assert her position. In assertiveness training this is called the "broken record technique." You repeat your position over and over again until you are understood. She also has accepted that it is her job to convince Greg about the true purpose of her efforts.)

Greg: "I don't know what to do. I really don't." (Greg finally believes Diane, but he can think of no helpful course of action. He has used up every idea he's had. So he does what's second best—admit this to Diane.)

Diane: "I have one idea. I'm not sure that we recognize when each other is hurt. How about if we develop some kind of signaling system that communicates our feelings nonverbally? I heard Dr. Berger lecture about this problem once, and he suggested that we hold up our hand in a stop gesture. He emphasized that we would have to respect this signal and refocus on the person's pain. It's much more complicated than I am explaining it, but it gives you some idea of what we could try. What do you think?" (Diane doesn't have any ideas either. But she has been searching for new information, and fortunately she picked up something in one of my lectures. She offers this as a proposal and investigates how Greg feels about this idea.)

Greg: "It sounds worth a try to me. But there are a few problems that I see in it. I'm not sure we know how to talk to each other without blame. I know that once you start blaming me for your feelings I react. I don't want to hurt you, and it upsets me whenever you suggest I do." (Greg is now sharing what he needs from Diane. If he were more honest with himself, he would be able to identify that sometimes he does want to hurt Diane. Many men and women are ashamed to admit this desire, and I believe they are much more likely to act out these feelings if they aren't able to own and identify these feelings. Diane doesn't want to encourage a solution that is contingent on how she behaves, so hopefully she will be able to spot this maneuver and gently suggest something more robust.)

Let's step back and look at what has happened between Greg and Diane. Diane approached Greg with the "we have a problem" attitude. He had some difficulty responding because it was out of the ordinary. He was used to their discussions ending up in blame sessions. Once he realized that Diane was sincerely trying to reach out to him, he responded positively. Sometimes it takes persistence and a strong desire to turn around a dysfunctional pattern in your relationship before you see the results. So how many times do you try this new behavior? As many times as it takes to get results or realize there is a better alternative.

Once he realized she wasn't blaming him, they began to search for solutions to their problem. He didn't have any suggestions immediately, but once she primed the pump he was able to join her in the search for a solution. Diane suggested a noninflammatory way they could communicate their hurt. Greg saw some difficulty in it and shared his reluctance. This couple had successfully begun a search for a mutually acceptable solution to their gridlock. The next step for them would be to refine and monitor their solution and appreciate each other's efforts.

Often a conversation between couples who are verbally abusive does not go this smoothly. The conversation that I described is ideal and is possible with some help from a skillful therapist.

Let's turn to a more typical problem and see how steps three to seven work.

Bill and Sally: *Fighting Fair*

$\mathcal{T}$he following situation often occurs in new marriages. A relationship is most likely to experience difficulty when a person is added or subtracted to the relationship. When a couple gets married, they are adding in-laws to their relationship. The couple needs to address this change and successfully adapt to the new situation if the relationship is going to stay healthy.

We will drop in on Bill and Sally, who have been married for only three months. Sally is angry with Bill's mother because she is rude to her. (Bill's mother is suffering from the empty nest syndrome and resents Sally for "taking" her youngest child.) Sally is upset with her mother-in-law's behavior, which has caused trouble in the marriage because Sally has tried to discuss the situation with her husband, who has avoided addressing Sally's feelings and concerns.

We are going to drop in on the middle of Bill and Sally's conversation. Sally has already turned to Bill and told him how upset she is. She has been paying a terrible price for the emotional tension: daily headaches and irritated bowels.

By sharing her concern in the following manner, Sally has enlisted Bill's cooperation by not blaming him for the difficulty she has had with his mom. Instead she has told him how much she loves him and needs his help in coping with this situation.

It is actually fortunate that Sally has lost her patience with her mother-in-law. Her tolerance permitted her to accept a situation that was unacceptable. Let's see what happens next between Bill and Sally as they attempt to find a solution to this challenge.

Bill: "I guess I didn't want to face how bad this situation was between you and my mother. I've always felt terrible about this whole deal. I'm not sure what to do to help you."

Sally: "What I need from you is your support. When your mother is out of line, I would like you to take the initiative and tell her. I'm always the bad guy. I'm the one who ends up setting the boundaries. Your mother sees me as controlling her access to you. I'm sure she thinks I'm the one who's responsible for the conflict. She doesn't see that she is out of line and overstepping her welcome."

Bill: "I know you two are having a problem, but I'm not sure I can support you in the way you are requesting. I think you are being too hard on Mom sometimes."

Sally: "It's hard to talk about this when you are speaking in generalities. Please be specific. When was I too hard on her?" (Sally has asked for Bill to be more specific. Speaking in generalities does not help to solve a problem. It only inflames it).

Bill: "All right. Last Saturday when my mom and dad came over for dinner, you didn't want Mom to help you in the kitchen. She likes helping out. Why couldn't you just let her make the salad or something like that?"

Sally: "What you didn't hear and what you often don't realize is that your mother takes every opportunity to tell me how you like your food prepared. I'm sick and tired of being told how to please you. I'd like to figure that out on my own, without your mother's instructions."

Bill: "But she is only trying to help."

Sally: "That's not the point. The point is that it is our house. I want her to treat me like an adult. I'm not one of her children. If she wants to give me a suggestion she should ask me if I want it, not just assume that I do. I want you to support me in setting some limits. You need better boundaries with your mother, too. I'm always the one saying 'No' to her. You don't dare to tell her 'No' about anything. You are too passive with her."

Bill: "I'm not passive. It's worse. I'm paralyzed."

Sally: "I want you to take a stand. Are you going to be my husband, or are you going to be your mother's son? I won't live with you sitting on the fence. It's too painful. I want you and I love you. I'll do anything I can to support you, but I need your support too."

Bill: "All right, I see your point. It's going to be tough for me, so I keep thinking I can talk you out of the problem, but it's not going to go away. I just don't think I can do this without getting some help. Maybe a therapist could help me figure out the best way to handle the situation."

Sally: "That sounds like a great idea. Probably we should both go. It's not going to be easy, but I am committed to our marriage and I want to find a way to address this problem."

In this scenario, Sally continued to assert herself and express what she needed from Bill. Bill was caught between his mother and his wife. He was unsure about where his loyalties should fall. He was confused and reluctant to confront the situation. While there was some emotional immaturity present in how Sally was internalizing her feelings about the situation, she still was able to begin a constructive discussion of the problem with her husband. If their relationship were more dysfunctional, Sally would avoid pressuring Bill altogether. She would try to "suck it up" and deal with this situation alone—which wouldn't work. Her resentment toward Bill and his mother would grow stronger and stronger. She would become more and more upset and continue to manifest these feelings in her medical problems, which would become worse and eventually require serious medical intervention. Sally would begin to try to control the relationship with Bill through her illness. He wouldn't stand a chance. The relationship would become gridlocked in a silent but deadly struggle.

Since Bill was paralyzed and Sally didn't know how to help him beyond what she had already done, the best alternative for them would be to get help from a family therapist.

John and Lucy: *In Search of Better Sex*

John and Lucy have been married for six years. In the beginning, they experienced intense passion. John is a very sensual and sexual person who loves sex and loves making love to Lucy. However, over the last two years, Lucy's interest in sex diminished. She used to possess the same passion and desire for sex as John, but something changed. She can take it or leave it. Lucy has not made an overture toward John in over a year. Her sexual appetite is nil.

John doesn't understand what has happened. He has tried to be patient with Lucy, but nothing has changed. His patience has given way to frustration. He doesn't know what to do. We join John and Lucy on a Sunday afternoon. Earlier that week John made a commitment to himself that he would broach this subject with Lucy today. Let's see what happens.

John: "Lucy, I have wanted to talk to you about our sexual relationship for a long time. I keep putting it off because I think things will change. They haven't, and I'm dissatisfied. I miss the kind of intimacy we shared earlier in our relationship."

Lucy: "I, too, have been feeling like we should be talking about this, but it's hard for me. I am glad you brought it up."

John: "I think another reason that I have avoided this subject is that I know it's a difficult subject for us, and I am afraid that it means you have lost your feelings for me: That you aren't attracted to me any longer. I'm afraid right now, even as I tell you about my fear."

Lucy: "I still love you, John, but something in me has changed. I just don't feel any interest in sex."

John: "I heard Dr. Berger say that the door to the bedroom opens off of the living room. Is there something going on between us that has been bothering you? I'd like to know if there is."

Lucy: "I've asked myself that question too. All I come up with is that I do harbor some resentment toward you for being what seems to me as 'selfish.' I hate using that word because it sounds so critical. What I am trying to say is that you seem to be more concerned with yourself than with me and my feelings."

John: "I didn't know you felt that way. Believe me, I don't want to treat you that way. Can you be specific?"

Lucy: "Well, let's take making love. I've told you that I enjoy oral sex. I want you to go down on me, but you don't. You seem to satisfy yourself, and then our lovemaking stops. Not once have you asked me what I would like."

John: "Not once have you told me what you wanted."

Lucy: "That's true too, but that is not the point. It's a valid point, and I'll talk about it later, but right now I am answering your question. You asked me to give you some feedback, and I am. Instead of listening to what I am saying, you are turning it around and making it seem like it's my fault. I can feel that I resent that too."

John: "You're right. I guess I am blaming you. It's hard for me to think of myself as self-centered. I don't like that part of myself."

Lucy: "It's not that I don't like how you take care of yourself. I do. That's one of the things that attracted me to you. I just want you to be more aware of my presence too. Don't throw yourself away for me. Just include me."

John: "I want to do that, but it's not all my job. You need to speak up too. But let's focus on what you are saying. When else have you experienced my behavior as selfish?"

Lucy: "Last year when I wanted to buy a new car. I told you how much I wanted a Ford Mustang. We went and looked at the Mustangs, and then later that week you came home with a Volvo. You said that it was built better than a Ford, and it would be safer for me and the kids. I was extremely disappointed, but I felt like I would be an ingrate if I told you I didn't want the Volvo."

John: "I never realized you felt that way about the car. You didn't say anything."

Lucy: "You're right. But you didn't consider what I told you about how I wanted the Mustang. I know that I've contributed to the problem too by keeping quiet, but at times I get discouraged."

John: "I've just assumed that you would tell me what you want."

Lucy: "I have told you, but when you don't acknowledge what I have said, I surrender rather than assert myself. We're different. It may be easy for you to tell me what you want, but it is extremely difficult for me."

John: "Honey, I am interested in what you want. I want you to be happy. How can I help?"

Lucy: (Starts crying.) "No one has ever showed an interest in what I want. It seems that my purpose in life is just to please everyone around me. I'm sick of it. I'd like to go away somewhere and just be by myself."

John: (Moves closer to Lucy.) "I am interested in what you want. I realize I haven't demonstrated my interest in a way that you can see, but that's because of my selfishness and ignorance. I am very interested in you, Lucy. And I am willing to work on this issue."

Lucy and John are off to a good start. They are having a very personal discussion, and Lucy is beginning to tell John about her resentment and what she wants in the relationship. John loves Lucy, but he hasn't faced how selfish he is and never realized how difficult it is for her to tell him what she wants.

Their discussion is a good example for you and your partner when you have a problem. Notice that Lucy and John are both working very hard to avoid blame. Their energy is expended toward illuminating what needs to be said, which is therapeutic. They both act as subject monitors and keep their discussion from veering off course. In addition, John's sincere desire to meet Lucy multiplies the therapeutic benefit tenfold.

Now let's drop in on Lucy and John one month later when they are discussing how the solution is working.

John: "We said that we would sit down one month later to see how we are doing. From my end of things I see some improvement. I am trying to be more conscious of you and what you want, and trying to create more of a space for you to tell me what you want. How do you think I am doing?"

Lucy: "I see improvement, and I appreciate your efforts. It's still hard for me to believe that you are as interested in me as you claim to be. I know that's silly to say, but it's what comes up for me."

John: "I'd like to know when you felt that way last."

Lucy: "Last week. I told you I wanted to make love. It was the first time I have felt this deep a desire for you in a long time. You were sarcastic about it and said, 'I don't believe it.' I was hurt and immediately I felt distance from you. I wish I could have talked to you about it at the time. Instead, I just felt petty."

John: "It will be great when you can tell me how you feel and what you want at the very moment you are experiencing those feelings. But you are telling me about your feelings right now, and that's progress. It's true I was sarcastic. I am still protecting myself from rejection. It's great that your feelings are changing, but I am so used to being hurt that I am afraid. But that's my problem, not yours."

Lucy: "I don't see it that way. Whenever either of us has a problem, it's our problem. We are in this together."

Lucy and John are doing an outstanding job. They have reviewed how their solution is working and what needs to be refined to keep their relationship on course. It is especially important to note how supportive they were of each other regarding each of their respective failures. This is a plus but not a requirement.

Instead of condemning each other for not being perfect, they both expressed support and appreciation for what was done. If they didn't get this encouragement from each other, then it falls on each of them to be self-supportive and provide it for themselves. I remind you to be the kind of partner you want to be, regardless of whether your partner expresses appreciation for your efforts or not. It is not his or her job to make you feel good about what you do in the relationship. You are an adult, and it is up to you to take responsibility for your actions and motivation and give yourself the praise and support you need.

I hope these steps will help you struggle with heretofore frustrating areas in your relationship. I'm sure these ideas will help you and your partner. Do not be discouraged if they don't have the desired effect the first or second or even tenth time you try them. *Changing a relationship takes persistence and patience.* Change occurs through a series of successive approximations. We try something new; it doesn't work out exactly the way we want it to, but we learn from the experience. We use this new information the next time we are confronted with a similar problem, and we improve and take another important step in our personal development.

CHAPTER 8

Dealing with a
Reluctant Mate

*He that will not apply new remedies,
must expect new evils. . . .*

—FRANCIS BACON (1597)

I hope that by now you have challenged many of your assumptions and ideas about your relationship, and that you have learned some new ways to struggle with your partner. New ideas can help, but there are going to be times when, regardless of your efforts, you will still be stuck and unhappy with the relationship. When you hit such an impasse, I urge you to seek professional help.

It is best if you go to therapy with your partner. No relationship problem is generated by just one

181

partner. Both of you helped create the problem, and both of you are needed to solve it. So if you are going to seek help for your relationship, invite your partner to join you. If your partner agrees, share your appreciation for his or her willingness. However, if your partner is unwilling to join you in therapy, do not fret; I have some suggestions that may help you bridge this gap. The good news is that it has been my clinical experience that most partners are more willing to participate in therapy than their initial attitude suggests.

How to Approach a Reluctant Partner

"How do I get my partner to join me for therapy? I've asked, and he refuses." If this is your experience, the first suggestion I have is to look at how you approached your partner. How have you extended the invitation? Are you somehow contributing to your partner's reluctance?

I know you are probably saying, "Me?? Why me? I am the one trying to save the relationship!" You may even feel like hurling this book across the room. After all, you are the "good" partner seeking help.

I recognize that it may be hard for you to put your disappointment or anger aside in order to have empathy for your partner. I understand how frustrated you must feel. You are in a difficult situation, and you feel powerless and helpless to change it.

You have only two choices: (1) to focus on yourself and explore what you can do to change the current situation or (2) to remain frustrated and disappointed and eventually fall out of love with your partner.

As I see it, the first choice is ultimately in your best interest. Even if your relationship doesn't work out, you can walk away from it knowing that you have tried your best to make it work. You have been the partner you wanted to be, regardless of how your partner behaved. This means that you have held on to yourself and maintained your integrity; you have honored yourself.

So step back and see if you can identify any of the following factors that may be contributing to your partner's reluctance.

Blaming Your Partner

Many people do not realize that their approach is critical and blaming. Listen to how Suzie approached her husband, Bill.

Suzie: "Bill, I want a good relationship with you, but we don't seem to be getting anywhere. I don't know what else to do. You won't even read Dr. Berger's book. We should get professional help. We are stuck."

Suzie didn't start out too poorly. First, she stated that she was really trying to do things that would improve the relationship, and it wasn't helping. Then she stated, "I don't know what else to do." Admitting her helplessness was positive. She was disclosing what she was experiencing in the here and now, honestly and authentically. Then, however, she makes a serious mistake when she criticizes Bill for not reading the book. Bill will get defensive at this point, and the discussion will become adversarial. The second mistake Suzie made in her approach to Bill is when she introduced the notion that "we should" get help. Whenever we introduce a "should" into the discussion, it becomes less personal. We create distance. The discussion of their personal desires is no longer between Suzie and Bill. Now an authority outside the relationship is required. Such an approach will not be successful.

Let's look at a better way for Suzie to speak to Bill.

Suzie: "Bill, I am really struggling with our relationship. I love you and want to find a better way to connect with you, but I am unable to do this alone. I need help. I want to see a therapist to see if he or she can help me become a better partner to you. I know I have a lot to learn. I need your help, too. I want to ask if you would join me to help me, too. Your feedback and observations about our relationship would be of value to me in this effort. I imagine that it may be hard for you to agree to see someone with me, and I understand that it might make you uncomfortable. I recognize these things, and it would mean that much more to me if you would agree to join me in therapy."

I hope the differences between these two approaches are obvious. Yet there are several important things that I want to highlight. First, in this second example Suzie was only speaking about herself and her need for help. She did not point any fingers at Bill; she kept her discussion focused on herself and what she needed. Second, she was vulnerable when she asked for help, a very important thing to do when approaching your partner. Third, she recognized that it would be hard for him, and she expressed an appreciation for his consideration. And finally, she indicated to him that he would be of value to her in this process.

I am not guaranteeing this second approach will work every time, because it won't. But it does have a much better chance than the first. This kind of invitation is attractive and can go a long way in evoking your partner's cooperation. The goal here is to influence your partner through attraction, not promotion.

A More Direct Approach

There are times, however, when a more direct tack might be more effective. "I don't like our marriage. I want to do something to make it better, and I want you to be willing to change, too. I'd like you to join me in therapy." The positive thing about this approach is that the person is personally communicating and telling his partner what he wants.

If you are near the end of your rope in your relationship, you may even need to escalate your position to the next level. Being firm, direct and willing to induce a crisis may be helpful. In such a situation you might say, "I insist that we get some help. If you don't, I will move out to give you some time to think about the importance of this relationship. If you decide you want to salvage our relationship, then you can join me in finding a therapist who can help us straighten out our difficulties. I refuse to live like this anymore." **Remember that when you change what you are doing, your relationship will change.**

If none of these suggestions work, then enter therapy alone and discuss the situation with the therapist. Make this the first subject you tackle in therapy and see if he or she can help you find ways to inspire your partner to join you in treatment.

I recall one situation where all it took was a phone call from me to the reluctant partner. Jim had told Eileen that he would never go to therapy. He viewed all therapists as charlatans who were just out for the money. Eileen was very distraught about

Jim's reluctance. She knew they needed help. They were growing apart, and she didn't want to lose him. But all of her attempts to bridge the ever-widening gap just made the matter worse. After listening to Eileen, I offered to give Jim a call. She agreed.

Jim was obviously surprised to hear from me. After introducing myself, I chatted with Jim about my perceptions of what was going on in their relationship. After we talked for about five minutes, he agreed to join his wife for one session.

What convinced Jim to give therapy a try? I told him that he would be able to evaluate the value of therapy in one session. If he didn't see any value, then I wouldn't charge him for the visit. I guess I made him an offer he couldn't refuse. He agreed and has been in therapy for over a year with remarkable results.

Psychological Barriers

Let's explore some of the psychological forces that create barriers such as Jim's. I hope this discussion will help you gain insight into yourself and also into your reluctant partner. You will be able to use your understanding to be more compassionate and encouraging with your partner.

Shame

One of the most common barriers to seeking help is shame. Webster defines shame as "a painful feeling of guilt, embarrassment or disgrace." For some people, turning to a therapist for help is a disgrace. Many reluctant partners have told me they were raised with the idea that you should never air dirty laundry in public. For them, having a personal problem is a weakness that they must hide. Needing help is equated with being a *personal failure.*

If your partner received this message when he or she was growing up, there is no recognition that having problems is a part of being human. A partner who is ashamed of having problems is in the difficult position of putting down his or her own humanity.

No human being has all the answers. We are all perfectly imperfect. Admitting this truth and seeking knowledge is the first step in accepting oneself and approaching therapy with an open mind.

Making a mistake simply indicates a lack of knowledge or experience. Failure is an event, not a person. Being ignorant is a temporary condition and can be remedied. People can be educated! Don't give up! There is hope!

False Pride

False pride builds another barrier for some partners. If your partner refuses to seek new information or self-knowledge, he or she is suffering from false pride which is limiting personal growth.

False pride occurs when a person tries to live up to false ideals. An example from my life should help clarify this concept. At one time in my life I felt proud of believing that I didn't need anyone's help; I glorified being independent. I mistakenly believed that not needing anyone was a sign of maturity. Needless to say,

I wanted to be mature, so I tried to act as if I were completely self-sufficient. I created an image based on the denial of my personal needs and desires.

As I write this I realize how much I turned life upside down. I must have been looking at life in a mirror so that everything I perceived was backwards: Black was white, right was wrong, good was bad, impervious was glorified, and human wasn't good enough. Wow, no wonder I was so screwed up!

After many painful and frustrating years, I started to develop a more realistic perspective. I began to see that the most important goal in life was to become more fully human, not perfect. I have devoted the last three decades to learning what it means to be human.

Fear

The final psychological barrier we will discuss is fear. Sometimes your partner is terrified that counseling may reveal deep, shameful secrets that have been buried since childhood. These types of secrets cover up violations so damaging that the person has even hidden the truth from himself or herself, yet still senses the shadow memory lying just below consciousness.

Such secrets may involve rape, incest or violent abuse. These traumatic acts damage children and make them feel shameful and worthless, feelings that continue into adulthood. If you suspect that your partner fears therapy, you can help by reassuring him or her that the primary purpose of counseling is to improve your relationship, not to assign blame, and that you wish to get assistance because you love your partner and want to spend the rest of your lives together. It is also important to reassure your partner that he or she is in control of when and what he or she addresses in therapy. No competent therapist will push someone to deal with an issue unless the person is ready and willing.

If you are unable to convince your partner to accompany you, go to a counselor alone and discuss your concerns about your partner. The counselor may be able to facilitate a meeting.

In conclusion, shame, false-pride and fear are often impediments to getting help. These barriers can be removed if the reluctant partner is able to become aware of how he or she is interfering with life. Invite and challenge your partner to move forward. Ask your partner to join hands with you as you both learn how to be stronger, more honest individuals, and wiser, more open partners. Great joy awaits you both.

Love is the most powerful psychological human force. Surrender yourself to it and all that it requires, and you will be forever changed. You will become who you were meant to be. You will be vulnerable, authentic, inspired, depressed, ecstatic, worried. You will know what it means to be of value to yourself and to someone you love. Enjoy the journey and remember— none of us ever gets it perfectly.

Some Final Thoughts About Relationship Matters

I hope you have discovered some helpful ideas among the preceding pages that will aid you in this never-ending journey.

Here are some final thoughts I want to share with you:

1. **We are all ignorant when it comes to relationship matters.** This is nothing to be ashamed of. It is a fact of

the human condition. Don't take yourself too seriously. As William Blake so eloquently stated, "If a fool would persist in his follies, he would become wise." Be outrageous! Face your ignorance! Accept it! Ask for help when you need it. Educate yourself. You can learn how to be a better lover, friend, husband or wife.

2. **We are all doing the best we can at any given moment.** Do not be harsh and judgmental when your partner fails to please you or does something that disappoints you. Be consoling. Search for the positive intention in all of your partner's behavior.

3. **Be proactive in your relationship.** When you run into trouble, stay focused on your behavior. Do not focus on what your partner is or isn't doing; it's what you are doing that must be your focus. Don't blame your partner. Focus on changing your behavior.

4. **Learn how to be assertive and tell your partner what you want.** Inform your partner about what you want instead of criticizing your partner for what he or she is not doing.

5. **Learn to welcome your successes and failures.** There is useful information in all of your experiences. If things are going well, learn from your success. If things are not going well in your relationship and you can't figure out what to do about it, get help. Don't wait.

6. **Challenge your expectations, identify your emotional dependency and learn how to take responsibility for your life.** Grow up and learn how to respect yourself

and your partner. I believe that most discord in intimate relationships can be traced to expectations that are ultimately created by emotional dependency. Our emotional dependency demands others to behave a certain way that will make us feel good about ourselves. If they don't cooperate, we either become enraged or depressed. When you grow up, you stop manipulating others to provide you with self-esteem. You become self-supporting through your own actions.

7. **Romantic relationships are built on a fragile emotional bond.** There are no guarantees that your relationship will be successful. The only thing that can come close to a guarantee is to cultivate a healthy pattern of communication with your partner. If you have a mutually satisfying and rewarding relationship, you have the best chance of creating a relationship robust enough to withstand the rigors and challenges inherent in coupling.

8. **Trying does count.** Remember, your effort to create a mutually satisfying relationship says a lot to your partner about your love. Positive results are a bonus, not a requirement.

Relationship Troubleshooting Guide

We all run into situations where we are not at our best in our relationship. It's unfortunate but true that we are oftentimes clueless when it comes to knowing how to bring out our best in the heat of battle. Sometimes we regress, acting childlike, pouting or throwing a temper tantrum. We have all done it at one time or another, and invariably we feel remorseful and embarrassed afterwards. Here are some suggestions for you that might help you gain perspective and meet these situations better in the future.

One important point that I want to make before I continue is that this is for you, not your partner! I am certain that I will discuss things that you would like your partner to try too, but do not bring these up, especially if you know you are right. At some future time, when you are not in the heat of battle, you may invite him or her to read a particular section to see if it might be helpful. But while you are in the heat of battle this kind of a suggestion will be misinterpreted to mean that you are telling them that they are the problem. Remember what I said: the emotional climate of a relationship is mutually determined; it's what you and your partner are doing that is causing the problem.

The other thing I urge you to remember is that the first few transactions in a discussion are most crucial. Dr. John Gottman's research demonstrated that the start-up of a conversation is critical. If you get off on the wrong foot it is hard to recover. It is much better to take the time and start up using the best of you. I will try and provide you with several different ways to get off to a good start in dealing with potentially difficult situations.

On Being Criticized

If you are feeling criticized, ask your partner if he or she would be willing to restate the feedback or complaint in a less critical manner. Assure your partner that you are interested in understanding his or her feelings, but it is hard for you to remain open when you feel criticized. Tell your partner that you need his or her help.

On Feeling Dismissed

If you are experiencing your partner as dismissing your concerns, take a deep breath and get centered before attempting to discuss the situation. It is best to begin by stating something like, "I know you care for me, so I imagine that what I am saying must be hard for you to hear by how you are reacting. If this is true, I would like you to talk with me about it." Or you might try, "It might just be difficult for you to relate to my feelings because you have trouble understanding them. I am not asking for you to do anything about my feelings. Ultimately that is my responsibility—not yours. I am asking you to try to put yourself in my shoes for the moment. Please see if you can understand what I am experiencing, and then we can talk about what to do about it later. I'd like to know if you are willing to try this." If he or she agrees, then proceed; if not, then don't push the issue. Say something like, "I respect that you don't want to try this right now, if at some point you change your mind, please let me know. This is really important for me." At which point you need to do something to soothe your own feelings like writing about what is going on, taking a long walk or a hot bath, or comforting yourself in a rocking chair.

On Feeling Hurt by Something Your Partner Said

Feelings are not right or wrong, but they are susceptible to misinterpretation and distortions. The first thing I want you to remember is that when you are hurt, your feelings are your responsibility, not your partners. Nobody makes you feel what you're feeling. You feel the way you feel because of how you perceive and react to the situation. The best way to discuss your reaction is to first check out your perception. Here is a format that I learned that might be helpful. First, identify what you are reacting to by saying something like, "When you stated that you didn't want me to join you when you go visit your friend"; then add what you imagined or made up about what they said. "I imagined that you didn't want me along because you don't enjoy my company." Next state what this caused you to feel: "I feel very sad to imagine you might feel this way." And finally ask for clarification: "Please help me understand what you meant by what you said."

Sometimes you might be correct in what you perceived. If this is the case, you have a very important discussion ahead of you; if it is not the case, then your partner's clarification should help. Unless, of course, that you don't believe that he or she is being honest with you, and if that is what you imagine—check it out.

Telling Your Partner That You Are Upset Without Causing a Bigger Fight

My first thought about this is that it may not be possible if you and your partner have an escalating pattern in your relationship. But here are a few things to try until you get more help in unraveling this destructive pattern.

Instead of telling your partner what you don't like, tell your partner what you want without criticizing. For instance, if he left the toilet seat up and you asked him hundreds of times to put it down you might say, "I want you to put the toilet seat down, and even though I have told you a hundred times I will tell you one hundred more times until you listen to me. I know you care for me. Will you please try harder?" And then let it go.

You can also start the conversation by saying something like, "I don't want to cause a scene with you, and if what I say is inflammatory please let me know, and I will try to restate my position in a softer tone or manner. I really want you to think of me every time you pee, and remember that I would love it if you'd put the toilet seat down when you finish." If you can't find a better start-up, then just own it by saying, "I am sorry I am unable to present this to you in a better way. I will get some help to see if I can find a better approach. I'd like to know if you have any ideas."

You Are Upset Because Your Partner Forgot Something That Is Important to You

Expecting your partner to read your mind is the cause of many problems in a relationship. Your partner cannot read your mind. Every relationship consists of a break-in period where you and your partner get to know one another. If you are both emotionally and psychologically present during this time, you will learn a great deal from each other by paying attention and learning from how your partner behaves and reacts. Your partner's nonverbal reactions provide you with a great deal of knowledge about what he or she likes, how they prefer to be touched, how they like to be kissed, how they like to be hugged, etc.

If you are in the early phases of your relationship, then understand that you are still learning about each other. The task is for you to help each other understand what is important. If your relationship is further along, then the problem is that your partner is not present, which means that you are also not present. Remember what I said earlier, that whatever you are experiencing in the relationship there is a counterpart in your partner. I tell the couples that I work with that you are in the same room, but in different corners.

So if your partner does not seem to know what you want and what you would like, it is likely that he or she has not been emotionally and psychologically present and that you have also checked out. Remember that when you change, the relationship has to change too. To turn this around, become present. Focus on what you don't know about your partner, get connected and learn how they want to be touched, kissed or held. Try to look at them with a new pair of glasses, as though you are seeing them for the first time. What do you see?

You can create change in your relationship by treating your partner in the way you want to be treated. Lead by example.

You Hurt Your Partner, and Your Apology Is Not Accepted

The first thing to contemplate is, are you really sincere in your apology? Saying something like, "I am sorry but I wouldn't have called you a fat ass if you hadn't criticized my driving," is not an apology. You are blaming your partner for what you said rather than taking responsibility for what came out of your mouth. If you approach your partner in this manner, they won't believe you are sincere—because you aren't. You are just making excuses for your rotten behavior.

The hallmark to an authentic apology is humility. You are not being humble if you are blaming someone else for your actions. Saying something like, "Regardless of what you said, I am sorry for how I behaved. There is nothing that justifies my hurtful comments. I am sorry for hurting you!" I hope you feel the difference in these two approaches. The latter is much more vulnerable, open and humble.

Cloe Madanes, a brilliant family and couples therapist, developed a highly provocative approach to therapy she called "Social Injustice Therapy." This method was developed in her work with family members who sexually violated another family member's personal boundaries. After much preparation the person who violated the victim and the family would apologize on their knees in front of each and every family member, acknowledging how they spiritually wounded the victim and family. If your partner is not accepting your apology, you may want to get down on your knees to apologize, and while you're at it acknowledge the spiritual wound that you have created. This can be a powerful experience for you and your partner. It will be tangible evidence of your remorse and sincere desire to make amends.

On Dealing with Resentment

If you are resentful about something that has happened in your relationship, then it means that you are going over and over something that has happened. Here is a useful approach to addressing your resentments.

Resentment indicates three things. First, that there is something unresolved between you and your partner—you need to make some kind of a declaration to your partner about what you resent. Second, root out the unexpressed demand. Finally, exchange the word "resent" with the word "appreciate" and make the same statement.

So here is how to apply this formula. First, turn inside and identify what your resentment is: I resent you for

_____

(*fill in the blank*). Next, identify the demand underlying your resentment, and then turn your demand into an appreciation. Here's an example.

Imagine that your partner criticized you for how you were dealing with the children when they were jumping on the couch, and this really upset you. You were up all night resenting his comment that you don't know how to discipline the children.

So you might say something like, "I resent you for criticizing me in how I was supervising our children." In the next step you might discover that underlying your resentment is an unstated demand like "Don't criticize me! You don't have a right to criticize how I raise our children because you are never home." The third step is to exchange the word "resent" with "appreciate." "I appreciate that you criticize how I am supervising the children; it shows that you care." If your partner is open to it, you can state your resentment and demand and appreciation directly.

Following these simple steps can help you resolve any resentment.

Wanting to Talk to Your Partner About Something Important and Not Knowing How to Start the Conversation

This is a common problem with a very simple solution. Whenever you are stuck, I want you to share *that* with your partner. Saying something like "I have something I want to discuss with you, but I don't know how" begins the discussion. The more specific, the better. "I have something I want to discuss with you, and I am afraid that I won't approach you well and we will end up in a fight. I don't want to fight with you. I want to talk with you."

Having a Hard Time Asking for What You Want Sexually

I am always amazed at how we suffer in silence in our relationships because we have trouble asking our partner for what we want. Remember I said that one of the most difficult things for you to do is to tell someone who is important to you what you'd like. The door to the bedroom opens off of the living room, so there is no surprise that we also have this problem during our most intimate moments with our partner.

The cure is simple. Discuss where you are at. "I want to ask you to do something, but I am embarrassed to tell you what I'd like" may open up the subject enough for you to be able to support yourself in asking for what you want. A few guidelines once you get the conversation moving are:

- Turn a general remark into something more specific. Change "I want to experiment with you tonight" into "I want to try something different with you tonight. I want you to tie me up and drive me crazy."
- Transform negatives into positive. Change "I don't like when you kiss me that hard" to "I want you to kiss me more gently. It really turns me on!"
- Change the past into the present. Instead of saying, "When you touched me that way I really liked it" to "I want you to touch me softly right now. I want to feel your soft touch right now."

Take this risk. It may open up a whole new dimension to your relationship and help you and your partner to start enjoying your sex life again.

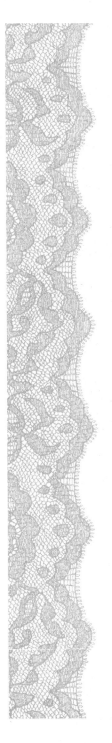

Cure Cards: Therapeutic Aids to Help You Communicate

In this appendix I have created a collection of Cure Cards. These aids are to help you communicate in the heat of battle, especially when you have lost your ability to stay focused on the solution. I want you to use these cards when you are stuck at an impasse and don't know what to do. Find the card that seems to relate to your situation, and show it to your partner. If I haven't provided you with a card for your particular situation, then make your own. Trying something new may help you and your partner break the gridlock. Remember, you cannot solve a problem with the consciousness that created it.

Please don't abuse these cards. They are

meant to help you find a solution. If you aren't sincere when you deploy one of them, you will defeat their purpose. These are not to help you win an argument or prove your partner wrong. They are to help you reconnect.

I am sorry.
Please be patient with
me; God isn't finished
with me yet.

Please help me; I am
feeling scared right now.
I need you to be more
gentle right now.

My pride is making it hard for me to tell you
I was wrong. I am truly sorry for hurting you.

I am very interested in what you have to say,
and yet I am having a hard time listening to you
when you seem to be so critical.
Please help me by restating in a less critical manner
what you want to say to me.

AHHHHHHHHHHHHHHHHHH!
I am frustrated and don't know what to say anymore.
Can we take a break and come back
in an hour to finish this discussion?

I know that I emotionally betrayed you, and
I am sorry. I will do whatever it takes
to address how I betrayed you.
I know that the solution begins by
being more present and responding to what
you want and need in our connection.

I want to make up with you.
I miss you.

I want to make mad and passionate love tonight.
Let's try something new. I have some great ideas!

I feel a lot of distance between us, and I don't want
to be distant anymore. I am not sure how
to reach out to you. I need your help.
I miss you. Please come back to me.

Ouch, that hurt!!!!!!!!!!!!!!!!!!!!!

I know we are out of synch right now. I have faith
that we will find our way back to each other soon.

I can hardly stand it when I see
that you are disappointed with me.
I don't want to let you down. I am sorry.

Let's stop quibbling. I want to focus on a solution.
Let's discuss some ideas.

You are more important to me
than I am able to express. I want you to know
that I have a difficult time
telling you how I really feel and being vulnerable.

I don't like what you just said. I feel hurt
and embarrassed. I want you to be
more considerate of my
feelings, please.

Index

Note: footnotes/notes are signified by n after the corresponding locator

skills, 54, 55, 76
styles of, 21, 55–60
unassertive, 112–114
compromise, 35–37
conflict in relationships
  avoidance of, 27–28
  compromise and, 35–37
  fear of, 101–103, 157–158
  resolution of, 5, 88
  "tit-for-tat" configuration and, 91
confrontation, 9, 88, 97–98
control, 138–144
cooperation, 9–11
couple's therapy, 122–123, 181–191
Covey, Stephen, 45
"Crimes of Love", 98–101
criticism, 25–26, 28, 69–70, 142, 194
cross-complaining, 83–84
cycle of abandonment, 4
cycle of emotional neglect, 5

D
denial, 101–102, 156
differences between partners
  acceptance of, 31–32, 165
  negotiation and, 65–67
  personality types and, 138–144
  respect for, 57–60, 81, 163
direct communication, 111–116,
  121–122
dismissal, 194–195
disrespect, 60, 116–117, 142–144
distrust, 63–64, 101
divorce, 4–6, 41, 136–137
dominance, 76–79
Dr. Phil, 45
dysfunctional relationships, 81–82, 129,
  134

E
emotional climate, 61–65, 127–145
emotional dependency. *see also*
  codependence

anger and, 52–54
approval and, 70
boundaries and, 133
communication and, 49, 110–111,
  116, 157–158
decreased sexual desire and, 83
demands for perfection and, 34
family of origin and, 24–25
intimacy and, 20, 24, 32
loneliness and, 30
love and, 20–21
low self-esteem, 52–53
people-pleasers, 12
reciprocity, 123
recognizing, 15, 91, 190–191
emotional maturity, 5–6, 69, 81, 152
empathy, 12, 21, 88–90
"emperor's new clothes" dynamic,
  101–102, 157
enabling, 155–158. *see also*
  codependence
expectations in relationships
  acceptance of differences, 165
  challenging, 190–191
  emotional dependency and, 110,
    111
  reciprocal behavior and, 20
  seven deadly expectations, 43–74
  suppression of, 8
  unreasonable, 15
extrovert, 138–139

F
faith, 63–65
false pride, 149–151, 187–189
family
  abuse in, 24–26
  adult children of alcoholics and,
    99–100
  Alanon and, 155
  alcoholism intervention and, 22–23
  emotional dependency and, 24–25,
    110–111, 113

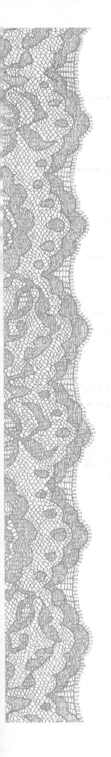

About Dr. Berger

Allen Berger, Ph.D., has been helping couples forge better relationships for more than thirty years. He enjoys an outstanding reputation as the "no-nonsense" relationship coach. He received his doctorate in clinical psychology from the University of California, Davis. He has trained family therapists throughout the United States and in Europe. He is in private practice in southern California.

Learn to make a love connection with any sign.

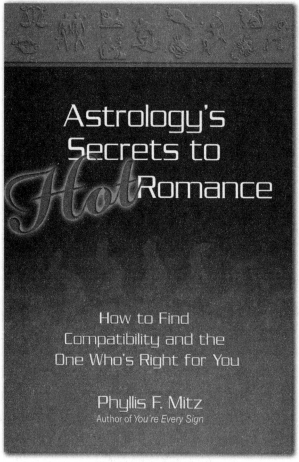

Astrology's Secrets to Hot Romance

How to Find Compatibility and the One Who's Right for You

Phyllis F. Mitz
Author of *You're Every Sign*

Code #4907 • $15.95

Astrology's Secrets to Hot Romance will guide you to the perfect sign for you.

What's your
Personal Passion Signature?

Code #2947 • $12.95

The Passion Principle delivers to-the-point
advice on how to improve and triumph in
relationships in love, life and work.

For a complete listing of titles or to order direct:
Telephone (800) 441-5569 • www.hcibooks.com
Prices do not include shipping and handling. Your response code is BKS.

Find out how simple truths can change everything.

Code #2414 • $14.95

Let the simple wisdom of the classic
children's story *The Velveteen Rabbit* start you
on your return to REAL.

For a complete listing of titles or to order direct:
Telephone (800) 441-5569 • www.hcibooks.com
Prices do not include shipping and handling. Your response code is BKS.